D0383305

DEDICATION

Fondly to Bill & Vieve Gore

and

Lovingly to my family: to my son, Alex, his wife, Kerry, and their children, Jack and Finn; to my daughter, Sophia, her husband, Matthew, and their children, William, Hugh and Peter; and to my dearest wife, Chris—all of whom have given deep meaning to my work and life.

"By my mid-career in the software technology industry, I wanted out. I knew I couldn't face another 30 years of the chaos that had become my industry and my life. Yet, I still had to feed my family, so I decided to make major changes. Since I was a VP of R&D, I had the authority to do so. Now the questions were: what, how, why? In that moment I realized that the problems I faced were not technological but human. I didn't need better people, but a better organization, a better culture.

I didn't just want to survive the rest of my career, I wanted to thrive and I wanted the people on my team to flourish. There were few books at that time that could have helped me figure it out, so much of my work was seat-of-the-pants, run-the-experiment, figure-it-out work. If you find yourself in a similar place in your current work life, you now have The Thriving Organization to not only inspire you, but guide you on your own journey to joy at work. Read it, and then take action. Your life will never be the same."

Richard Sheridan
CEO
Menlo Innovations

"Helping employees unleash their passion and talent at work can help any organization maximize its organizational and financial performance. The Thriving Organization provides deep insight and research into how teams and organizations create workplace cultures that achieve high engagement and exceptional bottom line results. Each chapter provides the understanding and tools necessary to transform your workplace culture into a high performance and highly effective organization. Every leader should read this to maximize their team or business success."

Kevin Ricklefs
Senior Vice President, Talent Management
CHG Healthcare

THE THRIVING ORGANIZATION

An EXPLORATION *into*
the DEEP DYNAMICS *of*
HIGH-PERFORMING
ORGANIZATIONAL CULTURES

MICHAEL PACANOWSKY

with
JIM McGOVERN

and in association with
**THE BILL & VIEVE GORE SCHOOL OF BUSINESS
WESTMINSTER COLLEGE**

**WESTMINSTER
COLLEGE**

**CENTER FOR
INNOVATIVE CULTURES**

The Thriving Organization
An Exploration into the Deep Dynamics of High-Performing Organizational Cultures
All Rights Reserved.
Copyright © 2019 Michael Pacanowsky
v4.0 r1.3

The opinions expressed in this manuscript are solely the opinions of the author and do not represent the opinions or thoughts of the publisher. The author has represented and warranted full ownership and/or legal right to publish all the materials in this book.

This book may not be reproduced, transmitted, or stored in whole or in part by any means, including graphic, electronic, or mechanical without the express written consent of the publisher except in the case of brief quotations embodied in critical articles and reviews.

Outskirts Press, Inc.
http://www.outskirtspress.com

ISBN: 978-1-9772-0219-2

Cover Photo © 2019 Sophia O'Brien. All rights reserved - used with permission.

Outskirts Press and the "OP" logo are trademarks belonging to Outskirts Press, Inc.

PRINTED IN THE UNITED STATES OF AMERICA

TABLE OF CONTENTS

PART I
The Thriving Organizational Culture:
Meeting the Challenges of the Twenty-first Century

PART II
The Thriving Organizational Culture

PART III
MOVING YOUR ORGANIZATION
TOWARD A *TO CULTURE*

PART IV
MINI-CASE STUDIES:
W.L. Gore & Associates, CHG Healthcare, and Menlo Innovations

ACKNOWLEDGMENTS

For much of my career, I was closely involved with W.L. Gore & Associates, the inventors of GORE-TEX® Fabrics and other break-through products—first as a consultant and then as a full-time Gore Associate. (Everyone who works at Gore is called an Associate.) Gore has been a very important part of my life, and so I want to especially thank my brother, David, who found Gore first and introduced me to this extraordinary company.

Through all my years at Gore, I had the opportunity to work with many amazing Associates. I worked briefly with Bill Gore (who died in 1986). I spent more time with Vieve, his wife and cofounder of the company, who would invite my children and me to her house when I visited in the summer. I worked reasonably closely with Bob Gore, Chuck Carroll, and Terri Kelly—all of whom served as Gore CEOs between 1984, when I first began a working relationship with Gore, and 2013, when I left the company. I also had the good fortune of working with thousands of Gore Associates in my 29 years with the company. I thank them all for their vision, their commitment, their integrity, their challenges to me, and their persistent work at making W.L. Gore & Associates a place where Associates could become their best selves at work.

I left Gore to accept the Gore-Giovale Chair in Business Innovation in the Bill and Vieve Gore School of Business at Westminster College in Salt Lake City. In that role, my charter has been to promote and extend Bill and Vieve's legacy in the business school's curriculum. I thank Ginger Giovale, Bill and Vieve's daughter, for her vision of having the school have a more substantial tie to her parents than just having their names on the building.

In 2014, I founded the Center for Innovative Cultures at Westminster. Our mission is "to help organizations thrive, by unleashing the talent, passion, and potential of people at work," a mission fully congruent with the vision of Bill and Vieve. In this endeavor, Jeanne Ambruster, a member and now chair of the Westminster Board of Trustees and a former Gore Associate with whom I had worked on many occasions in the past, has greatly supported me. John Sininger and Massimo Gilmozzi both former Gore Associates, have also supported me, as have Bob Henson, a longtime partner of the Center; Melissa Koerner, former dean of the Bill and Vieve Gore School of Business; and Steve Morgan, former president of Westminster College.

One of the upsides of the Center for me personally has been the opportunity to meet people from other extraordinary companies—often very different from W.L. Gore & Associates. This has caused me to try to ferret out what I call "the deep dynamics of high-performing organizational cultures." Scott Beck, Kevin Ricklefs, and Christine VanCampen opened the doors of CHG Healthcare to me and showed me how an organization with a very different strategic intent, and a very different culture, could still be a place where the organization thrived as the individuals in it flourished. I thank them for their willingness to share so much about what they do and how they do it.

I have also had the pleasure of learning from leaders at many other thriving organizations: Jerry Benson, former CEO of Utah Transit Authority; Randy Rasmussen, CEO of BioFire Diagnostics; Jeff Whiting and Ryan

Patano, cofounders of Alta Medical Management; Rich Sheridan and James Goebel, cofounders of Menlo Innovations; and Dave Durocher and Alan Fahringer, directors of The Other Side Academy.

I have learned much from academics and practitioners working in similar arenas. I would like to particularly mention Deborah Ancona, at the Sloan School at MIT; Sonja Sackmann, at the Bavarian Military Academy; Rod Collins with Optimity Advisors; Doug Kirkpatrick, formerly with Morning Star and now with NuFocus; Anna McGrath with Godfrey Dadich Partners; Dave Garrison with Profitable Engagements; Rudi Wimmer and Margit Oswald, with osb international; Steve Denning; Gary Hamel; Joseph Grenny; and the folks at the Center for Positive Organizations at the Ross School of Business at the University of Michigan. All of them provided stimulating discussions and points of view that furthered the development of the ideas in this book.

I also want to thank the readers of an earlier draft of this book who provided helpful comments for improvement: Robert Davison, Mike Dunham, Becky Fink, Ian Fitzgerald, James Hedges, Shana Hopperstead, David May, and Daniel Pandza.

The staff at the Center for Innovative Cultures helped keep the wheels on the bus as I navigated the task of writing: Susan Arsht, Michael Zavell, Summer Dawn Shumway, Taylor Rogers, Sarah Hirst, Brandi Workman, and Judy Fang. They were supportive and encouraging, and always an excellent sounding board against which to test new ideas.

Of course, I want to thank Jim McGovern, who brought his considerable skills as a business writer to this effort. Without him, I doubt I would have finished this book in my lifetime. And thanks to Sophia O'Brien, who conceived the cover and managed all the design work for the book.

Finally, I want to once again profusely thank Ginger Giovale, who, as the major donor to the Center, provided the encouragement and the financial wherewithal to allow me to undertake this task.

My deepest thanks to all of these folks, and others whose names I haven't called out here, for your faith in the value of this project.

INTRODUCTION

After graduating from college with a degree in English, I landed a job as a technical writer in a large engineering and aerospace company. It was the early seventies, and unemployment was the highest it had been in a decade, so I was glad to get the job. But I certainly had no idea how it would shape the rest of my life's work.

As it turned out, my new employer could well have served as a model of the classic bureaucratic, hierarchical—and as I soon learned, dysfunctional—organization. Time and again, my colleagues and I in the publications department found ourselves baffled by directives handed down from above that seemed to make no sense. They often had a negative impact on our ability to do our best work, and more often than not were changed within a matter of months—or even weeks—by yet another mysterious directive. At one point, I conducted an informal survey among the other members of my department, asking them how much of their capabilities they thought they were using in their work. The responses began at about 3 percent and topped out at 10 percent, a finding that left me disheartened but hardly surprised.

Our publications department, among other things, produced the company's monthly employee newsletter. At one point, I suggested to my colleagues that we survey our readers to find out what they liked and wanted more of. They liked the idea, as did our supervisor, and as did our department manager, who sent it up the ladder. About a month later, I got a call from one of the organization's senior executives. He thanked me for the idea but then said, "We're not going to do it." When I asked why, he explained, "Because if you do a survey, it implies that you might make a change based on what people think. To put it straightforwardly, we don't care what people think about the newsletter, and we're not going to change it."

That was pretty much the last straw for me. So, 13 months after starting, I hit the eject button and went back to grad school. Right from the get-go, I was driven to find out if there were organizations out there in which people did *not* feel like a cog in a mindless machine, where they used far more than that 10 percent of their talent—where they and the organization, together, actually thrived. What, I asked myself, would such an organization look like?

Eventually, and most fortunately, I found my way to W.L. Gore & Associates. In 1984–1985, I was on sabbatical from my role as an associate professor at the University of Utah, looking to pursue my interest in organizational cultures. My brother Dave, who worked at Gore, had often spoken to me about how Gore was a very unusual organization, so I asked him to make some introductions, and soon, with surprisingly little fuss, I was a participant observer in Gore's "eastern cluster."

It was immediately clear that Gore was different from my previous employer. Instead of feeling like a cog in a wheel, spinning furiously and getting nowhere, from my first month at Gore, I felt like I could actually get things done. Useful things that I and others saw as real and valuable contributions.

An example. Toward the end of my sabbatical, Bob Gore—the founder's son, who had taken over as CEO in 1976—asked me to give a talk to a group of leaders on what I had learned about the Gore culture during my stay. Rather than rely only on my own observations, I thought I should collect additional data, and since I had worked extensively with the HR team, I enlisted their help. The result ended up being 18 focus groups with Associates from the 11 plants in the company's eastern cluster, with more than 100 Associates providing input.

Nearly every group would begin with someone saying, "I really like working at Gore," at which point everyone would nod in agreement, and then the speaker would say, "but . . ." Then the pattern would repeat itself, with other Associates chiming in with their own positive experiences, often followed by some comment about how things were not perfect, and this or that in particular could be improved.

Even then, I remember thinking that this sort of conversation would never have happened in my previous company. No one there would have spoken so openly about our problems. But at Gore, people felt completely free to express their thoughts and feelings, both positive and negative. And the discussions never took on the tone of a "bitch session." Even the negative comments were offered constructively, in the spirit of "As good as things are here, we could do this particular thing better."

I presented the results to a group of 20–30 leaders, including Bob Gore, and Bill and Vieve, the company's founders, both of whom were still very much involved in the business. (Bill served as chairman until his death in 1986.)

At the meeting, I made clear my strong sense that Gore had a healthy, open culture where people felt empowered, committed, and glad to come to work every day—but I didn't hold back on the negative comments that had also come out of the focus groups. When I'd finished, the room was dead silent for a few seconds. Then, one of the leaders piped up.

"Mike, it's not that we haven't heard at one time or another pretty much everything that you've said here. The value in what you've done is you've put it all together for us in one place." And then what followed was an often animated discussion as the group tried to grapple with the issues raised by the Associates.

Finally, someone asked, "Well, what are we going to *do* as a result of what Mike has presented?"

You could feel that everyone was gearing up for action, at which point, Bob Gore said, "Right now, I don't think we should do anything. We don't know if we have a problem or not. Sure, the Associates in those groups made some negative comments, but Mike says the tone was generally very positive, and we don't really know how extensive or widespread the negative feelings are. I don't think we should act on something that may not be a problem."

With that, the discussion tapered off, and I went back to my office, noodling on how to help Bob and the other leaders get more clarity around the issues raised in my focus groups. Almost immediately, I thought of a survey, so I took the idea to the HR leader, then to Bob, and finally, to a couple of other leaders Bob suggested I talk to for their input—and just like that, with no fuss, we were ready to go.

With the help of the HR team, the survey was quickly rolled out to some 1,300 Associates in 11 sites, and then with the help of an Associate who was an expert in statistics, the data was analyzed, and a report produced. And so, in less than four weeks, I was able to go back to the leadership group with solid data validating my gut sense that the Associates' overall feeling about Gore and its culture was overwhelmingly positive, while the "negativity" that had surfaced in the focus groups was actually quite limited and focused in certain areas.

In addition to the findings themselves, what stood out for me was the fact that Gore could decide to conduct a survey on some pretty sensitive issues, develop and implement the survey instrument, compile the results, and get a group of key leaders together to discuss those results—in less time than it took my previous organization just to decide *not* to do a survey!

The difference between that experience, which no one at Gore seemed to think was unusual, and my previous corporate experience was night and day. I thought then, and 30 years later I still think, that there was definitely something special—something worth studying and worth emulating—going on at Gore.

Over the next decade, I consulted extensively with Gore. I turned my original survey into what became an annual survey of how Gore Associates felt about the culture. I led communication training workshops. I helped teams identify problem areas and possible solutions. I helped with team development. And, finally, in 1996, I became a full-time Gore Associate.

Like all Gore Associates, I was encouraged to find my "sweet spot"—to pursue work where my interests and capabilities aligned most closely with the company's goals and needs. With that in mind, I spent most of my time working on projects that were intimately concerned with the company's culture and how it manifested itself in matters of organizational change and development, leadership, decision making, communication, team effectiveness, strategy development, and so forth.

In 2013, I left Gore to teach in the Gore School of Business at Westminster College, and to launch the Center for Innovative Cultures, dedicated to "helping organizations thrive by unleashing the talent, passion, and potential of people at work." The good news is that a growing number of organizations are already doing so. These organizations thrive by enabling their people to thrive. While such Thriving Organizations may differ in many respects, particularly regarding specific practices, there are significant similarities in their core cultures, their fundamental assumptions about people, their values, and their operating principles.

ABOUT THE BOOK

This book is divided into several sections. In the first section, we'll examine the concept of a Thriving Organization. We generally capitalize the term (sometimes abbreviated as *TO*) to make it clear that we're talking about organizations that thrive not only in the sense of achieving their strategic intent and desired business results but also in the sense of enabling their people to thrive both personally and professionally. In this section, we'll also introduce you to three Thriving Organizations —CHG Healthcare Services, Menlo Innovations, and W.L. Gore & Associates.

These are three very different organizations. CHG Healthcare is a service business, placing doctors, nurses, and other healthcare professionals in temporary and permanent positions. The country's largest provider of *locum tenens*, or temporary physician staffing, CHG has some 2,500 employees in eight offices in six states, generating annual revenues of more than $1.5 billion. CHG is driven by what some writers have termed "customer intimacy." Its success depends on its employees' developing strong and lasting relationships with medical professionals on the one hand and hospitals and clinics on the other. And despite the company's deep and proven commitment to securing and acting upon its employees' input, CHG is unabashedly hierarchical in structure.

Menlo Innovations is a developer of custom software. Founded in 2001, the company has always been committed to being a business based on what its founder, Rich Sheridan, calls the Business Value of

Joy. Located in Ann Arbor, Michigan, the company remains small, with some 40+ employees and $5 million in revenue, but it's one of *Inc.* magazine's "5,000 Fastest Growing Companies in America," and it's been recognized by Forbes as one of "America's Best Small Businesses."

From its inception, Menlo has practiced a form of "extreme programming." Unlike the typical software development organization, Menlo staff work collaboratively—in pairs that change every week—in a large, open, and sometimes noisy space, with the CEO sitting in their midst. Rather than becoming specialists in a particular programming language or type of software, "Menlonians" (as they call themselves) routinely work on projects that are completely new to them, learning on the fly. The company's approach is so unique that new customers may initially be taken aback, but they are invariably delighted by the quality of Menlo's work. If you measure software quality by how well it works and how rarely it fails to work, it's worth noting that the last time software designed and developed by Menlo provoked a "software emergency" was in 2004.

W.L. Gore is a global enterprise, with more than 10,000 employees, offices in more than 25 countries, and manufacturing operations in the U.S., Germany, the UK, China, and Japan. Annual revenues are around $3 billion, from a wide array of products for application in the medical, fabric, pharmaceutical and biotechnology, oil and gas, aerospace, automotive, mobile electronics, music, and semiconductor industries. The holder of over 2,000 patents, Gore was once deemed by *Fast Company* magazine "pound-for-pound, the most innovative company in America."

From the start, Gore prided itself on being a flat organization, or to use Gore's own terminology, a "lattice organization." The company used almost none of the typical corporate titles—no directors, VPs, SVPs, and so on. And as indicated by the lack of titles and a traditional org chart, decision making was explicitly and widely shared.

In the above paragraph, and throughout the book, I've typically used the past tense when referring to Gore. That's because the W.L. Gore depicted in this book is the W.L. Gore I worked with for so many years. As of this writing, the company has been going through a period of substantial change. Some longstanding practices have been modified; several new leaders, including a new CEO, have been named. It's too early to tell the effect of these changes on the Gore culture.

Yes, these three companies differ in many respects. And yet, as different as they are, all three are Thriving Organizations, not only in terms of their sustained growth and outstanding financial performance but also how their people feel about the work they do and how they demonstrate their commitment to the company's success. High engagement and low attrition characterize all three. Gore and CHG have perennially been named to *Fortune* magazine's list of the 100 Best Places to Work.[1] Menlo is regularly named to the WorldBlu list of Most Democratic Places to Work, and has been recognized as one of the 10 happiest places to work on the planet by Denmark's "Chief Happiness Officer."

In short, these companies have thrived by enabling their people to thrive. That means that these organizations not only allow their people to *be* their best selves at work, they help them *become* their best selves at work. And that makes them worth a very close look.

So, once again, in the first section of the book, we'll talk about what we mean by a Thriving Organization, and we'll examine the business case for such organizations. We'll take a look at the concept of organizational culture—a closer look than you'll typically find in the business

---

1   In 2018, Gore did not make the Forbes list, after making it for the previous 20 years. How much this is due to changes going on in the company and how much to changes in how the list is compiled is unclear.

literature these days, where the term gets bandied about as if we all know what we mean by it, which I don't think is the case.

In the second section, we'll lay out the model of a "Thriving Organizational Culture" that my colleagues and I at the Center for Innovative Cultures have developed. We'll examine how this "iceberg" model is shaped by its underlying axioms, values, and principles, illustrating the discussion by examples drawn from CHG, Menlo, Gore, and other Thriving Organizations. Along the way, we'll also point you to some of the sources on which our ideas are based.

But what if your organization doesn't fit this model? What if your organization is *not* a Thriving Organization? How do you change the picture?

In the third section of the book, we'll take a stab at this crucial question. We'll look at what it takes to achieve lasting organizational change. We'll examine what it takes to overcome the organizational inertia and outright resistance that any major change initiative provokes, and we'll challenge the prevailing notion that successful organizational change requires a burning platform. And we'll lay out a set of working principles that you can adapt and apply to help your people and your organization thrive.

The final section of the book consists of mini-case studies of W.L. Gore, CHG Healthcare, and Menlo Innovations, each going into some detail about how the culture in each of these Thriving Organizations is manifest in specific practices and artifacts.

And now, with all that said, let's get started.

PART I
THE THRIVING
ORGANIZATIONAL CULTURE:

Meeting the Challenges of the
Twenty-first Century

WHAT IS A THRIVING ORGANIZATION?

When we talk about a Thriving Organization in this book, we're talking about an organization that is successful in two ways—one, regarding meeting its organizational challenges and achieving its strategic objectives; and two, regarding enabling its people to be and become their best selves, personally and professionally.

One way to think about this is to use what I call the Thrive-Thrive Matrix:

Figure 1. The Thrive-Thrive Matrix

The Individual

	WILT	SURVIVE	THRIVE
THRIVE			
SURVIVE			
WILT			

The Organization

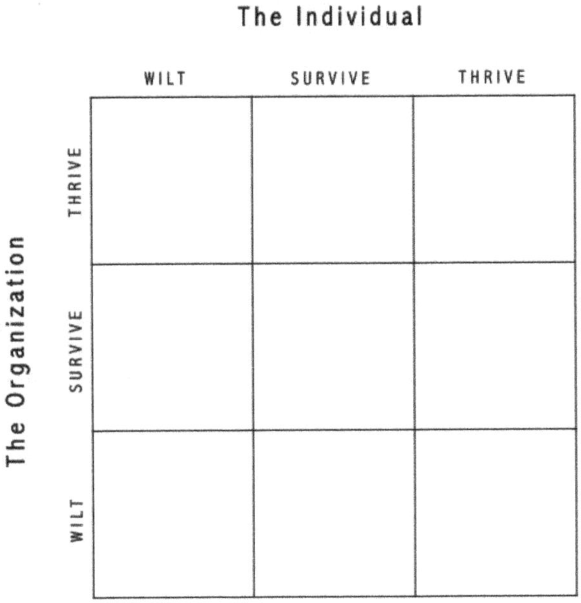

An organization that is thriving is making its numbers, it's growing, it's competing successfully, and it's positioned to go on growing and succeeding for at least the foreseeable future. An organization that is surviving is doing just that—surviving. It may be muddling along, with a few years of struggle followed by a few years of success followed by a few more years of struggle. It may not be facing an immediate existential threat, but without some dramatic change in how it does business, it's hard to see it being consistently successful over the long term. And as for organizations that are wilting, it may be that new technologies, products, or market dynamics have overtaken their business models, thus rendering them obsolete, or it may just be that hungrier, more efficient competitors have overtaken them. But whatever the cause, these organizations are not going to make it.

As for individuals, "thriving" in this context means that work is more than just a way to pay the bills. People who are thriving experience their work as an opportunity to grow, to do something meaningful, and to contribute. If they won the lottery, they might not keep coming in to the plant or the office—although a Gore Associate in Phoenix reportedly won the lottery *twice* and still remained at Gore!—but typically, they enjoy the work they do, the people they do it with, and the environment they do it in.

And this goes beyond having fun. CHG, for example, is a fun place to work, in the sense that almost every day brings some celebration or party, large or small. But what CHG employees say really matters most to them is that the company cares about them, that it gives them a chance to develop their talents, and that the work they do—placing doctors and nurses in places that otherwise have trouble attracting medical professionals—makes a real difference in the world. In a very real sense, they *care* about the work and the organization. As I said earlier, thriving in this sense means that the work and the organization help them become their best selves.

Menlo Innovations speaks to this sense of thriving when they talk about "joy." They are clear that joy isn't unmitigated happiness. There are rough spots. There are challenges. There are days when things don't go right. But the overall experience of working at Menlo is one of joy. Of growth. Of contribution. Of opportunity.

By contrast, people who just survive at work are pretty much there for the paycheck. They do what is required of them, enjoy what they can, and look to other areas of their lives for real satisfaction. That's not necessarily bad. These folks may just have other priorities in life. But at least for the organization, it may be less than optimal.

And as for the people who are wilting, these folks derive little satisfaction and certainly no joy from going to work every day. Maybe they're bored by the work, angry at their boss, disdainful of their organization's leaders, and cynical about its mission, but in any case, for these people, work is a painful experience.

These categories line up quite well with those typically used in discussions of employee engagement. Thriving individuals are likely to be *engaged*: their emotional connection to the organization and the work they do results in their regularly bringing something extra to the job. Surviving individuals are likely to be *disengaged*—doing their job, and often doing it well enough, but rarely, if ever, going beyond the job requirements. And the wilting individuals? These are the *actively disengaged* people who do just enough to keep their job while complaining, dragging their feet, letting others carry the load, and generally sucking the energy out of the organization.

Just as our concepts of individuals' wilting, surviving, or thriving line up well with discussions of engagement, our concepts of organizational wilting, surviving, or thriving align quite nicely with research done by Christopher Worley, reported in his book *The Agility Factor*.[i]

Worley looked at the financial performance of 80+ publicly traded companies over a 30-year span. While noting that no company outperformed the stock market every year, he found that about 18 percent of the firms consistently—at least 80 percent of the time—outperformed their market segment. These are the "thrivers." Conversely, 13 percent of the companies performed below the average for their segment about 80 percent of the time. (It's amazing that these "wilters" could have been around for 30 years!) The other 69 percent of the companies went through repeated boom-or-bust cycles, sometimes thriving, sometimes wilting. These "survivors" seemed unable to sustain and build on short-term success.

The point of the Thrive-Thrive Matrix is that there are many combinations of wilting, surviving, or thriving. You can certainly have an organization that is wilting—not meeting its financial or other key objectives—and in which the individuals in it are also wilting. Some of the department store giants of the past (Sears, JC Penney, and others) likely fall into this category.

You can have an organization that is thriving but in which the individuals are wilting—although, in today's highly competitive environment, it seems to me that such an organization will have trouble sustaining its success, especially if the job market is healthy and their best people can walk out the door. Amazon, with its high-pressure work environment and the high attrition rate among recently hired employees, might be such an organization.[2]

You can even have an organization that is wilting, but in which the individuals are thriving. The best example of this may be the dot.com wonder companies of the late '90s, where the people loved their work and their work environment, but the companies ultimately collapsed

---

2   See *Inside Amazon: Wrestling Big Ideas in a Bruising Workplace*, J. Kantor and D. Streitfeldaug, *NY Times*, August 15, 2015.

when they failed to meet the expectations of their investors and couldn't get successful products out the door.

And finally, you can have what we mean by Thriving Organizations, where both the organization and its people thrive together. And here is where we would place our three exemplar companies: W.L. Gore and Associates, CHG Healthcare, and Menlo Innovations.

A couple of other comments are in order about the Thrive-Thrive Matrix. First, the matrix is meant to be illustrative, not a perfect descriptor of where any particular organization might be. There are gradations within each category, different degrees or levels of thriving, surviving, and wilting. Organizations and certainly their people can and often do move across these dimensions, even in and out of categories. An individual who has been surviving moves into a new role, gets excited by the training, likes her new co-workers and team leader, and soon finds herself feeling much better about the work and the organization. She becomes engaged; she thrives.

And, of course, the cycle can go the other way. It seems safe to say that no organization is always thrive-thrive. There will always be ups and downs for the organization as a whole and for individual members, but in a Thriving Organization, the prevailing sense is that the organization is achieving its core purpose and that even when things are not perfect, it remains a great place to work.

So now, to be clear, let me reiterate the central tenet of this book. I believe strongly that it's possible to have Thriving Organizations—organizations that succeed in achieving their strategic goals while (and in my view, *because*) they also enable their people to become their best selves. The organization thrives, and its people thrive.

I also believe that at this particular moment in history, such organizations offer unique advantages. Let's look at that next.

CAN TWENTY-FIRST-CENTURY ORGANIZATIONS THRIVE— OR EVEN SURVIVE—USING A NINETEENTH-CENTURY MODEL?

Organizations exist to achieve some particular purpose—to make money, win wars, educate students, cure diseases, and so on. To achieve those purposes, their leaders, members, and other stakeholders have a vested interest in the organization's doing certain things as well as possible—and in the case of for-profit organizations, doing them better than the organizations with which they compete. In other words, they have a vested interest in maximizing performance.

But the longer an organization exists, and often the larger it gets, the more complex its activities become, and the more difficult it becomes to achieve and sustain the desired high level of performance. In the world of business, that challenge first became acute in the nineteenth century, when the Industrial Revolution made it necessary to transform a largely uneducated rural population into armies of factory workers who could generate, at the lowest possible cost, a river of products flowing uninterruptedly day after day, month after month, year after year.

To meet that challenge, the new manufacturing enterprises adopted and adapted the hierarchical organization model that had worked effectively for military forces since at least the days of the Roman Legion. New educational institutions like the École Supérieure de Commerce de Paris (founded in 1819), the University of Pennsylvania's Wharton School (1881), Harvard Business School (1908), and others provided a theoretical underpinning to the model and trained an emerging class of professional managers to make it work. And it did indeed work.

As in the military, a leader at the top, advised by a close circle of advisors, made all the critical decisions. Those decisions were pushed down the chain of command to latter-day centurions who made sure that the worker/foot soldiers on the production line carried out the tasks the decisions required. Thanks to Frederick Taylor, those tasks were broken down into simple, repetitive activities that required little—and ideally, no—creativity or initiative from the individual workers, who were, for all practical purposes, truly cogs in the machine.

By its clear designation of roles, responsibilities, and decision prerogatives, and its deeply entrenched command-and-control approach to leadership, this model enabled the modern corporation to channel and coordinate human energy very efficiently to achieve desirable organizational outcomes. As Figure 2 indicates, the hierarchical, bureaucratic model was also effective in generating a general level of prosperity that the world had never before even imagined.[ii]

Figure 2. Historical *Per Capita* Annual World GDP

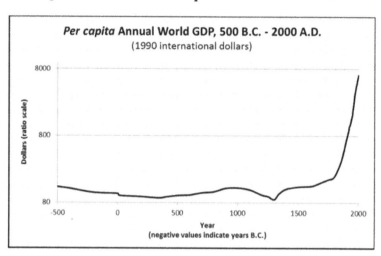

What we see in Figure 2 is that for most of human history, *per capita* GDP was flat. There was a small uptick at the time of what we call the Renaissance in the 1500s. And then suddenly, around 1780, roughly the beginning of the Industrial Revolution, the graph turns sharply upward. An even greater upturn takes place in the mid-1800s, which coincides with the advent of the railroads and the mills that signaled the advent of the modern corporation.

The problem is that times have changed, but most companies (and also most not-for-profit enterprises) are still trying to make do with the traditional model—and for the most part, that's not working very well.

Consider Figure 3, which shows the return on assets and the return on invested capital for all U.S. organizations since the mid-1960s.[iii] As you can see, 1960s' return rates of between 4.2 and 6.2 percent have now declined to slightly more than 1 percent.

Figure 3. U.S. Return on Investment for the Last 50 Years

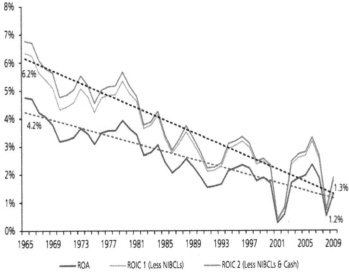

Source: Compustat, Deloitte analysis

And then there's the issue of productivity, which is closely related to our society's ability to provide widespread improvements in the standard of living. As Figure 4 indicates, U.S. productivity growth through the 1980s and mid-'90s showed a downward trend; then it spiked up until shortly after the turn of the century, before heading generally down.[iv] Current productivity growth is running at only 0.5 percent. That's not the only cause of the income inequality issue that's challenging us as a nation, but it certainly doesn't help.

Figure 4. Recent U.S. Productivity Growth

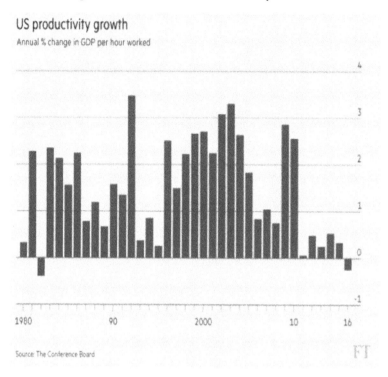

US productivity growth

Annual % change in GDP per hour worked

Source: The Conference Board

The fact is that today's world is significantly different from the nineteenth and early to mid-twentieth century when the hierarchical, bureaucratic organization was birthed and grew up. The modern corporation was made to leverage the thinking talents of the few to design work for the many so that the "doers" could reliably repeat essentially the same routine actions over and over again to generate significantly greater output than had previously been achieved by individual craftsmen working essentially alone.

But today's companies operate in a far less predictable world, a so-called VUCA world—volatile, uncertain, complex, and ambiguous.[3] The explosion of new technologies has driven disruptive innovation, hyper-accelerated the flow of information, and created a global business environment in which organizations are increasingly interconnected, where unknown competitors can blindside even the largest enterprises.

Back in 1967, Horst Rittel, a physicist-turned-city planner, made an interesting distinction between two broad classes of problems. *Tame problems* have a right answer and finding it is the stuff of analysis, a matter of breaking the problem down into small, solvable parts. With *wicked problems*, on the other hand, there is no "right" answer. Wicked problems require what is now called design thinking—designing an effective, workable, or elegant solution, given the constraints and resources involved.

So, another way of understanding the current predicament of many traditional hierarchical organizations is that they were built to solve tame problems, but increasingly, the VUCA world they now operate in is increasingly serving up wicked ones!

And on top of all that, today's organizations are drawing on a workforce that has changed significantly over the past 100+ years. In 1910, the proportion of the U.S. labor population that had graduated from high school was 13 percent. The proportion of college graduates was just 3 percent. With a workforce with that level of education, it's not all that surprising that an organization's leaders might think it was obvious that they—the presumed "smartest guys in the room"—should

---

3   The VUCA acronym was introduced by the U.S. military to describe the environment in which today's troops must operate. In response to the challenges posed by this environment, the military has adapted its leadership approach to give more authority and autonomy to the troops on the ground. Ironically, many commercial enterprises are still wedded to the command-and-control mentality that the military is changing!

make all the decisions. And for a long time, that seemed to work.

But by 2013, almost 90 percent of the U.S. workforce had a high school degree, and almost one-third had a college degree. Not surprisingly, those better educated workers are increasingly disaffected by the underutilization of their knowledge and talent. They are—to use a term that certainly never existed in the nineteenth or even the early twentieth centuries—*disengaged.*

At best, only 30 percent of the American workforce today is actively engaged at work. That is, only 30 percent are excited to go to work on Monday morning

Jim Keane, the CEO of Steelcase, often begins his presentations with a slide with the single figure 70 percent on it. He explains that this represents the percentage of U.S. workers who are not actively engaged at work and notes that the numbers on engagement have not changed appreciably in all the years that Gallup has been conducting its surveys. He then goes on to say that, given the virtually unchanging low percentage of engaged employees over many years, "One can only conclude, then, that American organizations are *designed* to create disengagement."

because they are confident that by using their commitment, creativity, and initiative, they can make a difference. Only 30 percent have a sufficient emotional connection to their organization that they work with passion, that they will, on their own, make an extra effort to help the organization succeed. The other 70 percent are TGIF folks doing a job and collecting a paycheck, and of that group, 20 percent are *actively disengaged*—so bored and disenchanted that they intentionally screw things up in acting out their frustration. (And these dismal U.S. figures are significantly *better* than what's happening globally.)

These issues are likely to grow even more challenging as younger generations of workers—the Millennials and Gen Z folks—come into their own. While there appear to be important differences between these generational cohorts, they share an insistence on doing work that they feel passionate about, in organizations that allow them to exercise significant autonomy and give them ample opportunity to grow professionally.

In today's hypercompetitive environment, companies need to react more quickly to potentially dangerous change. Better yet, they need to anticipate those changes, to see them coming down the road in time to adapt appropriately. In many cases, the people best able to see those changes coming are the people closest to the customer; the people best able to identify solutions are the people closest to the product and service. By and large, those are not the people at the top of the hierarchy.

But if many of those people in the trenches are disengaged, what chance is there that they will exercise their creativity? What chance is there that they will think about what they see "out there" and how it will affect the organization that pays them?

Senior execs who worry about declining productivity, lack of innovation, and potentially existential threats from hidden competitors, are increasingly coming to understand that the traditional organization isn't built to foster the kind of engagement that can make the difference between success and disaster. Faced with this realization, many of them are now asking: How do we tackle this problem? How can we create an organization that thrives by enabling our people to thrive? Where can we find examples to help us meet this challenge?

WHY DOES IT MATTER? THE FINANCIAL IMPLICATIONS

In almost every discussion I've ever had with business leaders about Thriving Organizational cultures, at some point, someone will say something like, "Yeah, sounds good. But what about the bottom line?" For many people, there seems to be a clear, obvious logic to the idea of a working environment that allows and encourages people to give more of their discretionary effort, to take ownership for their impact on organizational outcomes, and to be passionate about innovation, customer service, efficiency, and effectiveness. But for those who "need to see the numbers," there is considerable hard data to suggest that Thriving Organizational cultures contribute to business success.

Gallup, for example, has published countless studies that show the positive effect of engagement on retention, absenteeism, innovation, and customer service—all of which impact the bottom line. Similarly, the Great Places to Work Institute has studies showing the positive bottom line impact of being a great place to work and business performance. (These studies also tease out the reciprocal effects—how great business performance makes it easier for an organization to afford a great culture.)

One of the most careful studies of the impact of Thriving Organizational cultures on business performance comes from the work done on "Firms of Endearment." Wegman's, 3M, Google, IBM, FedEx, L.L. Bean, Patagonia, UPS, Marriott, Southwest Airlines, SAS, BMW, Honda, IKEA, Unilever, W.L. Gore—these are some of the 70 or so companies cited in *Firms of Endearment: How World-Class Companies Profit from Passion and Purpose*.[v] If we're looking for examples of how some organizations are built to thrive, this is a very good place to start.

In 2007, Raj Sisodia, Jag Sheth, and the late David B. Wolfe—two professors and a highly regarded consultant—published the first edition of *Firms of Endearment*. The authors and their students had begun by asking people, "Tell us about some companies you love. Not just like, but *love*," a process that yielded hundreds of names. They applied an array of qualitative and quantitative screening questions to that list; e.g., "Would most people say the world is a better place because this company exists? How extensive a track record have they built? Do they have intensely loyal customers? How high is their employee turnover?"

That initial screening cut the list to 60 U.S. companies, and over the next two years, they took an in-depth look at each of those companies, including extensive interviews with all major stakeholders, finally ending up in the first edition with 28 companies. For the second edition, in 2014, the authors cast a wider net, ultimately focusing on 72 "firms of endearment," or FoEs—28 publicly traded U.S. companies, 29 privately held U.S. companies, and 15 non-U.S. companies (13 public/2 private).[4]

These companies are different in many ways. Given their differences in size, geographic reach, customers and markets served, products and services delivered, not to mention how long they've been in existence, it's inevitable that they would also differ in organizational structure, leadership style, and many other characteristics. They all, however, ". . . meet the functional and psychological needs of their stakeholders

---

4   See Appendix 1 for the complete list.

in ways that delight them and engender affection for and loyalty to the company." It's important to note here that the authors are explicitly referring to *all* stakeholders—not just the owners and/or *shareholders*, but also the employees, customers, suppliers, and the communities in which they operate.

More specifically, what do these FoEs have in common? They espouse a purpose that goes beyond (although it certainly does not preclude) making money. While they may be more or less hierarchically structured, they "operate at the executive level with an open-door policy." They pay their executives less than their industry counterparts, but they pay their employees more, and invest more in training and in "creating a nurturing work environment." They "project a genuine passion for customers" and "treat their suppliers as true partners."

The results? Well, their employee turnover is significantly lower than industry norms. Their "marketing costs are far lower than their competitors, while customer satisfaction and retention are far higher." And their financial performance is exceptional. For example, ". . . the stock price performance of [publicly traded] FoEs has dwarfed the S&P 500 over three, five, ten, and fifteen-year periods." That sounds like thriving to me.

One more point.

In their attempt to differentiate FoEs from other companies, the authors of *Firms of Endearment* point directly to culture: "This [culture] is what most sets FoEs apart from the crowd and enables them to create greater value for *all* their stakeholder groups." Going further, they maintain that: "The passion, energy, dedication, generous spirit, and expansive creativity found in every FoE are all products of their culture."

This suggests that we'd better take a close look at the concept of organizational culture.

IT'S ALL ABOUT CULTURE

It seems like a safe bet that how to make companies more efficient and more productive has been an issue virtually from the birth of the Industrial Age. Many, although certainly not all, of those early mill owners undoubtedly wanted to squeeze as much out of their workers as possible. They might not have put it this way, but they certainly wanted to "optimize organizational performance" as much as any twenty-first-century CEO.

Given the traditional adherence to a hierarchical, command-and-control organizational model in which a relative handful of leaders make all the critical decisions, it's not surprising that the issue of leadership itself has always been of great interest. For the longest time, the key questions have been: What skills and personal traits does it take to make a great leader? And just as crucial, How do you develop great leaders?

The rise of professional business schools, with their advanced degrees in business—the MBA mainly, along with such business-focused degrees as the Masters in Finance—was one response to the ongoing quest for leaders who could make the right strategic decisions and then manage their organizations effectively to implement those decisions. Launched in the early twentieth century, these degrees became especially popular in the century's latter decades.

Consider this shift. In 1970, MBAs accounted for 11.2 percent of all master's degrees conferred in the U.S.—compared to master's degrees in education, which accounted for 37.2 percent. By 2011, business degrees accounted for 25.4 percent of all master's degrees, compared to education, which accounted for 23.6 percent.[vi] This shift was undoubtedly driven by organizations' quest for higher performance, which, in turn, drove a need for higher performing leaders—and, in turn, led to higher levels of compensation for business leaders. You can make a lot more money as a business executive than you can as a teacher!

While the quest for improved leadership continues to be of great importance to most organizations, in recent years other issues have risen to prominence. Since 2013, Deloitte has conducted a global survey of top business leaders to identify their most pressing concerns. In 2013 and 2014, leadership was far and away at the top of the list. In 2015, however, leadership and "culture and engagement" were tied at the top of the list. In 2016, "organizational design" topped the list with 92 percent of respondents citing it as Very Important/Important, followed by leadership at 89 percent, culture at 86 percent, and engagement at 85 percent. And as Figure 5, taken from the 2017 report shows, the conversation continues to evolve.[vii]

Figure 5. What Keeps Leaders Up at Night 2017

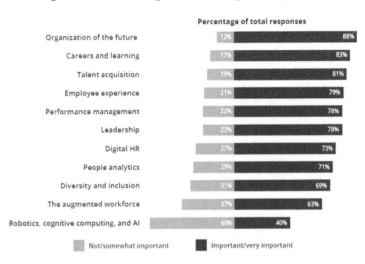

Percentage of total responses

	Not/somewhat important	Important/very important
Organization of the future	12%	88%
Careers and learning	17%	83%
Talent acquisition	19%	81%
Employee experience	21%	79%
Performance management	22%	78%
Leadership	22%	78%
Digital HR	27%	73%
People analytics	29%	71%
Diversity and inclusion	31%	69%
The augmented workforce	37%	63%
Robotics, cognitive computing, and AI	60%	40%

What seems to be developing is a growing realization that to improve organizational performance, we need to do more than simply focus on leaders. We need to look at our organizations in a broader context. More specifically, we need to look at organizational culture. This culture includes, is shaped by, but is not limited to the organization's leadership model and the specific decisions and actions of its leaders. It's this broader culture that drives engagement and ultimately performance. (This seems like the appropriate moment to reference Peter Drucker's often cited—although impossible to verify—comment that, "Culture eats strategy for breakfast.")

OK, but what *is* organizational culture?

As we continue to explore what it means and what it takes to be a Thriving Organization, we'll do so from this broader cultural perspective. But first, it seems like a good idea to define what we mean by culture in an organizational context. Many discussions of this topic leave the term undefined, as though we all know what it means and we all mean the same thing when we use it, but I don't think this is true.

For some, culture means values—"what we believe in." For others, it means practices—"how we do things around here." Edgar Schein, for many years a distinguished professor of Organizational Development at the MIT Sloan School of Management, is widely credited with having introduced the concept of organizational culture into the lexicon. In his 1985 book, *Organizational Culture and Leadership*, Schein defined the term as:

> "... *a pattern of shared basic assumptions that was learned by a group as it solved its problems of external adaptation and internal integration, that has worked well enough to be considered valid, and therefore, to be taught to new members as the correct way to perceive, think, and feel in relation to those problems.*"[viii]

Schein's model of organizational culture, often referred to as an *Iceberg Model*, consisted of three levels. Above the waterline are the organization's visible practices, structures, and processes. Below the waterline are strategies, goals, and philosophies that may or may not be known to the organization's members, as well as implicit, taken-for-granted beliefs, perceptions, thoughts, and feelings.

Figure 6. Schein's Iceberg Model of Culture

Schein's model is compelling because it points to the profound challenge facing leaders who want to emulate the culture of organizations other than their own. In too many such cases, the leaders focus on what is visible, on the organization's practices and artifacts. Company X has high levels of engagement and great performance, and it offers free food in the cafeteria, on-site massage services, and flexible work schedules, so if we do the same, we should get the same results.

Unfortunately, it's not that easy. Because so much of what constitutes a culture lies below the visible surface, and because a culture is based on past learnings specific to each organization, trying to transplant practices and artifacts from one culture to another, without understanding and integrating the underlying assumptions, beliefs, values, and principles, is like trying to transplant a flower from one geography to another without knowing anything about the environmental conditions in both places. Success is hardly guaranteed.

A Few Key Points about Organizational Cultures

- Every organization has its own unique culture.
- Culture links how we perceive, feel, and think to how we act.
- Culture has its own architectural integrity, so cutting-and-pasting "best practices" may not yield desired outcomes.
- Culture infuses everything. Culture can help or hinder the organization in its strategic intent.
- Culture is dynamic, evolving, and open to new interpretations.

We've seen that today's organizations operate in an increasingly interconnected, global, and technology-driven world—a complex, unpredictable environment characterized by ever-accelerating change, an environment that demands a greater than ever capacity for organizational agility and creativity. To succeed and even survive in this dangerous new world, they need to tap into the potential of people at every level of the organization, not just a relatively small number of leaders.

Unfortunately, the hierarchical, command-and-control organizational model that grew out of the very different conditions and needs of the nineteenth and early twentieth centuries isn't really built to meet this new need, as indicated by the fact that so many people working in such organizations—people who are far better educated and knowledgeable than any other workforce in history—are disengaged at work.

In the quest for a better model, the focus has broadened from what kind of leaders we need to what kind of organizational culture might produce better results. And that poses the question of whether we can identify the common assumptions, values, and principles that would constitute the culture of a Thriving Organization, even though the specific practices might be quite different from one such organization to another.

I think the answer is Yes.

PART II
THE THRIVING
ORGANIZATIONAL CULTURE

THE THRIVING
ORGANIZATIONAL CULTURE

For the past several years, my colleagues and I at the Center for Innovative Cultures have worked to develop a model of the organizational culture that appears to manifest itself consistently in Thriving Organizations.

At the risk of trying your patience, let me say again that by a Thriving Organization, we mean one that succeeds in achieving its most important strategic and financial goals, while at the same time, the people who work there grow and make full use of their talents to become in a real sense their best selves. Equally important, we believe firmly that these organizational and personal/human outcomes are deeply inter-related: the organization thrives *because* its people thrive, and its people thrive *because* the organization creates the conditions that enable them to do so.

The Model of Thriving Organizational Culture (or *TO Culture* model) that we've developed is drawn from a wide variety of sources. It draws on academic research; on the extensive literature on leadership and organizational practices produced by both scholars and business leaders; on my own three decades with W.L. Gore & Associates, as well as experiences that my colleagues and I have in working in and consulting with diverse organizations; and from the contributions of business leaders and scholars from across the globe who have participated in the Center's many activities and events. (For a more extensive discussion of some of the sources we've drawn on, you might want to check out Appendix 2.)

In working on the *TO Culture* model, I've stress-tested the ideas and insights of these many diverse sources by reflecting on my own experiences with W.L. Gore & Associates. I've asked myself, "Does this insight help me make sense of my experience at Gore? Does it seem true to my experience?" And as I've spent more and more time with Thriving Organizations other than Gore—organizations like CHG Healthcare Systems and Menlo Innovations—I've broadened the question to "Do these ideas seem true for all of these Thriving Organizations, not just Gore?"

The answer is yes. Not that any organization follows every aspect of the model all the time, but these Thriving Organizations, and many others, are more rather than less likely to be characterized by adherence to the model.

Finally, let me repeat: our model is a synthesis of many familiar ideas. What is new about the *TO Culture* model is the unique synthesis that it represents. I believe that by developing this synthesis—and illustrating it as we do in the following pages—the model offers a fresh and useful perspective on what it takes to create Thriving Organizations.

So, with all that as background, here's our model of the Thriving Organizational Culture.

Figure 7. The Thriving Organizational Culture Model

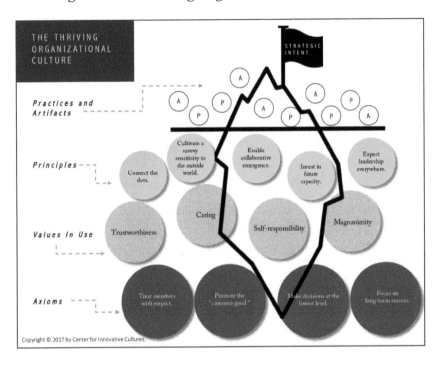

Before we move on to an up-close look at the model and its various components, we should note that the lack of specific artifacts and practices reflects the fact that the underlying principles, values-in-use, and axioms that shape a Thriving Organization can and do manifest themselves in many different ways at the practice level. As suggested earlier, the three firms we are looking at most closely—W.L. Gore, CHG Healthcare, and Menlo Innovations—are, on the surface, very different kinds of organizations. Their workplace environments look different; their organizational structures look different; their ways of compensating, developing, celebrating, and evaluating their employees are different—and yet, as we will see, the principles, values-in-use, and axioms that lie below the surface of their cultures are quite similar.

That brings me to that Strategic Intent flag so conspicuously planted on the summit of the *TO Culture* model. It's there because we start from the assumption that for an organization to thrive, its culture must be in service to the strategic intent of the organization.

There is, to my mind, a somewhat simplistic argument between those who believe that culture is preeminent, and those who believe strategy is preeminent. On the one hand, the people who believe that "Culture eats strategy for breakfast" suggest that if you focus first on culture, the right strategy will inevitably follow. On the other hand, you have renowned academics writing articles with titles like "Culture Is Not the Culprit," arguing that focusing on culture is the wrong thing to do when an organization is in trouble. (I would point out that "culture" is pretty much left undefined in both arguments, and a richer definition of culture—like Schein's—would be a helpful starting place for the discussion.)

Anyway, for me, it isn't culture or strategy, one or the other. If your strategy stinks, a great culture isn't going to save you. And if your strategy is great, but a disengaged workforce won't execute on it, you'll sub-optimize for sure. The question is: how does the culture support or not support the strategic intent of the organization—and likewise, how does the strategic intent leverage the culture?

Often expressed as a mission statement, an organization's strategic intent is its reason for being. Made explicit, it can and should serve as the organization's True North.

When an organization's strategic intent is well known, it provides employees, customers, partners, and shareholders with a common ground that transcends business, function, region, and individual agendas. It can, or at least should be, the ultimate arbiter of different opinions, a way of integrating different perspectives around a higher cause.

So that's why we planted that Strategic Intent flag atop the iceberg in our model.

As to the principles, values, and axioms that we've included in the *TO Culture* model, they are clearly not meant to be comprehensive. A cursory review of the academic and business literature surfaced some 80 different principles that could rightly be associated with a thriving organization. But ultimately, in the interest of simplicity, we chose to include only five, in part, by combining similar or closely related principles.

The same is true for values and axioms. For example, we could certainly have added more values-in-use to the model than the four we ultimately selected. In addition to *trustworthiness, caring, self-responsibility*, and *magnanimity*, how about integrity, honesty, creativity, respect, customer focus, transparency, accountability, fairness, collaboration, or teamwork? But again, we opted for simplicity.

Our decision to significantly streamline our model—to include only a limited number of core axioms, values-in-use, and principles in each layer of the cultural iceberg—reflects our interest in making the model more useful to leaders facing the challenge of actually building a thriving culture, rather than a more academic interest in making the model comprehensive. That said, we do believe that the elements we've included, taken as a dynamic whole, fairly represent the essential components of a Thriving Organization culture.

Let me make another point about the layers and elements that constitute the model. It's important to note that they are mutually supportive, both vertically and horizontally. For example, going across at the axiom level, the imperative to treat members of the organization with respect in some sense leads to and certainly supports the axiom that decisions should be made at the lowest level. Going up, the *treat members with respect* axiom leads the Thriving Organization to place a high value on self-responsibility, which, in turn, supports such principles as connect the dots, enable collective emergence, and expect leadership everywhere.

And finally, it must be said that no Thriving Organization will fully and consistently manifest even our selected list of cultural axioms, values, and principles. But we do believe that more often than not, Thriving Organizations—the ones we discuss in this book and others—bear significant and obvious similarity to our model.

Okay, with all of that out of the way, now let's explore the iceberg of a *TO Culture*.

STARTING AT THE TOP

Let me confess right here that this chapter involves a bit of bait and switch. My experience tells me that most people who are interested in creating a Thriving Organization want to get right to the practices and artifacts that manifest themselves in such cultures. They want to know how a Thriving Organization looks and operates differently from their own organization. I understand the desire to start at the top of the *TO Culture* iceberg and say something about its visible practices and artifacts.

On the other hand, there's a real danger in focusing first at this level, because doing so may reinforce the belief that starting with practices and artifacts is how you go about building a *TO Culture*, whether from scratch or through a process of culture change. That idea is flat-out wrong.

As I indicated earlier, *trying to carry over specific practices from one organizational culture to another, without carefully thinking through the assumptions, values, and principles that underlie those practices, is not a recipe for success.*

The point is that the particular practices and artifacts of any Thriving Organization are based on the principles, values-in-use, and axioms that lie below the surface of its culture, and must be aligned with the organization's strategic intent, the industry it operates in, and the business model it follows. That's why those practices can and should differ from one Thriving Organization to another.

Rich Sheridan, CEO and cofounder of Menlo Innovations, touched on this point the very first time I visited with him. He pointed out that a steady stream of visitors comes through Menlo every year—several thousand visitors in a typical year. These folks are determined to learn about how Menlo operates and how they might use those learnings to improve their organizations.

But as Rich indicated, right away most of those visitors grab onto what's most obviously different at Menlo. They're fascinated by the fact that Menlo's workplace is one large, open space. No offices (except for three glass-enclosed conference rooms), even for the CEO, and no cubicles. Everyone works at moveable tables, which are moved around every week. Looking at this space, which is, by the way, usually much, much noisier than their own workplace, the visitors are drawn to the way the walls are covered with sketches, posters, notes, ideas, project status information, and more. And they are very deeply interested in the fact that Menlo's software developers work in pairs—and that those pairs change every week!

As Rich told me, Menlo's visitors all too often seem to think that if they go back to their own organization and rip down the cubicles, let everybody put stuff on the walls, and put everyone to work at tables, they will soon have a Menlo-like culture, along with dramatically improved organizational performance. But as Rich himself learned when he first tried to build a "culture of joy" in his previous company, that's not the way it works.[ix]

So here's where the bait and switch comes in. Rather than at this point going into the matter of *TO* practices and artifacts, I'm going to ask you to be patient. I promise that in the following chapters, as we work our way through the axioms, values-in-use, and principles that are critical to any *TO Culture*, I will definitely include some examples of how these are manifest in actual practices and artifacts.

And then, when we really have a handle on what lies below the surface of a *TO Culture*, and when we've examined the challenge of how to move an organization toward such a culture, we'll look more closely at the day-to-day practices of W.L. Gore, CHG, and Menlo Innovations.

Trust me: this is the way to go.

THE *TO CULTURE:* PRINCIPLES

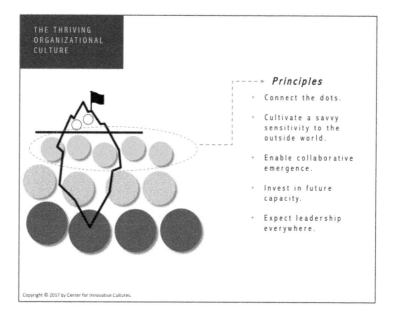

The man who grasps principles can successfully select his own methods. The man who tries methods, ignoring principles, is sure to have trouble.

Ralph Waldo Emerson wasn't talking about organizational culture when he wrote those words, but he might as well have been.

In any organizational culture, there's always a set of principles at work, a set of general guidelines that drive the development of day-to-day practices and artifacts. That process may not be conscious. Suppose, as is often the case, an organization's leaders don't realize that the values on its website are different from the values-in-use. (They may not even have thought about the issue.) In that case, the principles at work in the organization—and the practices they shape—will still align with the values-in-use, not the espoused values.

If, for example, a manufacturing company proclaims that it places a high value on quality, but its production processes consistently allow defective products to go out the door, employees will quickly figure out that the real value in use is maximizing output, not quality, and they will act accordingly. And the resulting disconnect between the company's espoused values and its actual practices will prove a sure recipe for employee cynicism and disengagement.

But the point is that whether or not they are consciously applied, in any culture there's always a set of principles at work, guiding the choice and development of the organization's practices and artifacts.

In a Thriving Organization, these five principles are necessarily involved:

- Connect the dots.
- Cultivate a savvy sensitivity to the outside world.
- Enable collaborative emergence.
- Invest in future capacity.
- Expect leadership everywhere.

CONNECT THE DOTS

As we've seen, in organizations based largely on the traditional, bureaucratic model,[5] each person's role and actions are carefully scripted with an eye to producing a maximum efficiency of effort. Regardless of how much their leaders may say they value employee initiative, employees in such organizations are not really expected or encouraged to think independently as much as to follow the prescribed plan. As Henry Ford famously lamented, "Every time I hire a pair of hands, someone wants to bring their brain along as well."

The mid-twentieth-century job enrichment movement tried to help employees understand the broader context into which they and their work fit. But that broader understanding wasn't generally tied to greater empowerment. The real operating principle was still "Do your job!"

But as we've discussed, "just do your job" no longer works as well as it once did. In today's world, where change is the only constant, employees—many of whom have more frequent and honest contact with the organization's customers, vendors, and partners than any of its executives—are very likely to be periodically confronted with something new, something not covered by the prescribed rules. If their organization operates largely in command-and-control mode, their response to such situations is likely to be "run it up the ladder." And more often than not, the issue will keep getting kicked upstairs until it arrives on the desk of someone with sufficient hierarchical rank to decide what to do. Not necessarily a bad model, I suppose, except that it takes time (which is precious), and it often leads to decisions made without a real sense of the facts on the ground.

---

5   With all the technological, economic, and other changes that have occurred over these past several decades, and with all the discussion of how organizations need to adapt to the resulting disruption, it's probably hard to find many organizations that are still operating on a "pure" traditional model, but many still follow the fundamental assumptions of the traditional model.

In a Thriving Organization, that's not how things work. There, the assumption is that the environment *will* throw curve balls, and when it does, the people in the best position to figure out what to do will probably be those closest to the situation. At the very least, their input will be incredibly valuable.

Based on that assumption, leaders in a Thriving Organization believe that it is imperative for decisions to be made at the lowest level. They value not compliance but self-responsibility.

The question then becomes, how do you help people make good decisions? At least part of the answer is by connecting the dots, making sure that employees across the organization have a clear sense of the big picture—of the organization's strategic intent and how their particular work fits into that picture. But how do you do *that*?

Many organizations have mission-vision-value statements. Many of these same organizations have monthly, quarterly, or annual all-hands meetings where the CEO discusses strategic objectives, financial performance, upcoming initiatives, new product introductions, new marketing campaigns, etc. Thriving Organizations (and admittedly, some that don't meet our definition of a *TO*) go further, consistently putting in time and effort to ensure that employees see the connection between these high-level issues and what they themselves do every day.

Sometimes, this process of connecting the dots poses its own challenges. At Gore in the late '90s, for example, there was a push to improve the performance of various enterprise functions—IT, marketing, finance, HR, and so forth. As part of this initiative, each function wrote its own mission statement, which was then reviewed by the cross-functional team working the project.

Most of the initial mission statements went something like, "Our goal is to be a world-class IT function." Only after considerable discussion did the lightbulb go on—the understanding that these aspirational statements connected the dots in the *wrong* way. As one Associate put it, "Hang on! As an enterprise, we make money by being a world-class product innovator, not by having a world-class IT function, or HR function, or even a world-class engineering function."

Ultimately, those functional mission statements ended up being revised to something more like, "Our mission is to provide the outstanding IT support necessary to help the enterprise be a world-class product innovator." That's different, and it can lead to different decisions down the road, from "Our mission is to be a world-class IT function." It connects the dots more accurately.

To get back to how leaders connect the dots in Thriving Organizations, they consciously and consistently seek to clarify the underlying causal loops that lead to good or bad outcomes. They provide a clear, strategic narrative that essentially says, "This is our business model. This is how we make money or don't make money. This is how we should be making choices about priorities regarding money and time. And this is how what you do every day fits in." And they work at this all the time.[6]

This point about making sure that people understand not only the organization's purpose and values, but also its business model and financial realities is critically important, even for non-profits. Without an understanding of the organization's current and projected financial situation, including its challenges, and a clear sense of what actually brings in money, it is extremely difficult for people to make—or even to appreciate and accept—realistic choices among alternative courses of action.

That's why high-performing organizations are typically committed to high levels of financial transparency. At CHG, Scott Beck goes on

---

6   You might want to check out www.engageforsuccess.org, a UK-based website focused on employee engagement, for an interesting discussion of how to create a compelling strategic narrative for your organization.

a "road show" at least once a year, and more often if need be, visiting all of the company's offices to explain and answer any question the employees may have about the company's financial performance, how it is doing compared to plan, and how it is doing compared to its competitors.

At Gore, financial information was shared on a monthly basis, to ensure that the Associates were clear about how the company made money and how their own work contributed to its success. With this understanding, Associates tended to have a good sense of value-added activity versus non-value-added activity, and a corresponding preference for doing value-added work.

At Menlo Innovations, they practice "open book management." Once a week, the entire team is invited to gather and discuss the company's key performance metrics, by week, month, quarter, and year. The goal, as COO James Goebel says, is to help every Menlonian "think like a business owner." Frequently, someone will suggest tracking some new metric to see if that information might help improve performance. If the team agrees, the new metric will be tracked for several months. If it does indeed prove useful, it stays; if not, it's dropped.

One night while I was visiting the University of Michigan, some folks from the business school took me to Zingerman's Roadhouse, one of 13 enterprises that comprise the Zingerman "Community of Businesses." The Zingerman culture is highly regarded for helping its people thrive, and one of my dinner companions that night had written a case study on the subject. To illustrate how Zingerman uses open book management, he asked our waiter, "How much money will the Roadhouse take in tonight?" The waiter replied, "Well, I *should* know that, but I've only been here three weeks, so I can't tell you and be sure I'm right. But I *can* tell you exactly how much I need to collect from each patron so that I break even on the night." And he told us. I'm happy to say that our table beat the spread.

The process of connecting the dots, including but not limited to the organization's financial model, has to go on all the time, at every level. Managers and supervisors and team members need to be connecting the dots as part of their everyday discussions about their work. "Here's how to make sense of our world and your role in it, so you can know how to make the greatest contribution to our collective success."

Here's another important point: the organization's leaders need to know what the dots are before they can connect them! They need to know what's going on in the employees' world. As obvious as that may sound, all too often the leaders who expound on their organization's strategic objectives and plans for achieving them seem, at least to the employees, to have no clue about what really goes on in the organization day in and day out. And again, that kind of disconnect leads more often to disengagement than engagement, and more often to cynicism than to commitment.

That's why leaders at Gore, CHG, Menlo, and other Thriving Organizations make sure to get in the trenches on a regular basis. Bill Gore was famous for wandering around every Gore plant, talking to the folks who were actually developing and manufacturing product. Rich Sheridan at Menlo sits at a table right in the middle of the bustling Menlo workspace, just like everybody else. CHG's leaders are similarly right in the middle of the workplace, and they meet one-on-one with employees all the time. And they all spend as much or more time listening than talking.

An excellent example of how an organization got serious about connecting the dots appears in *The Engaged Enterprise: A Field Guide for the Serving Leader*, by Joseph Patrnchak, the former Chief Human Resources Officer at Cleveland Clinic.[x] Patrnchak describes his experience leading a culture change at this world-renowned hospital system. One of the most important steps the organization took was to recognize and celebrate the fact that every employee had an important role to play in delivering a world class patient experience.

This critical change in perspective was captured in the phrase, "We are all caregivers." Not just the doctors and nurses, but everyone was a caregiver. The person in accounts receivable who helped a patient deal with insurance issues was a caregiver. The painter who kept the hospital rooms and hallways looking well-cared-for? A caregiver. The valet parking guy who greeted the patient and his or her family with a smile and words of encouragement when they pulled up in their car? Again, a caregiver.

To begin the process of embedding this "We are all caregivers" mindset in the Clinic's culture, all 43,000+ employees met in groups of 8–10 to discuss how their work fit into the overall "Cleveland Clinic Experience" of patients and their families. These were cross-functional groups, comprised of employees from across the enterprise, from the folks working in the kitchens and laundry to the physicians and executives. Once everyone had gone through this initial program—a process that took nearly a year—managers at every level were trained and supported in continuing the discussion on a regular basis in their team meetings.

The result of this sustained, connect-the-dots process could be seen in the Gallup employee engagement surveys conducted at the Clinic. Over two years from the launch of the initiative, the employees' rating on the survey item, *The mission or purpose of my organization makes me feel my job is important,* rose from 3.8 on a 5-point scale to 4.23—a very significant statistical increase.

And then, as Patrnchak noted, there was the anecdotal evidence, such as the financial analyst who commented:

> *". . . even though the finance group has no direct patient contact, information we provide can still affect the experience and outcomes*

of our patients." And this, from a member of the media group: "Even though we are in a nonclinical field, we strongly believe we are tied to the Cleveland Clinic experience . . ."

So, just to make the point one more time: if you want your organization to thrive, you'll want to take the time and the necessary steps to know what the dots are and connect them for the people who work in your organization.

CULTIVATE A SAVVY SENSITIVITY TO THE OUTSIDE WORLD

I believe that as human beings, most of us truly thrive only when we engage widely with the world. I believe that's just as true for introverts as it is for extroverts. I also believe that the same is true for the organizations we build and belong to.

Today, when information is the life blood of business, when information is more widely available than ever before—when, in fact, we sometimes seem to be drowning in it—too many organizations still limit the information on which they make decisions by looking inward more than outward. Yes, they invest in market and customer research, but they don't tap into the broad, deep ocean of information to which their employees have access.

In a Thriving Organization, on the other hand, one of the core principles shaping behavior is the necessity of "bringing the outside in," or as we put it in our *TO Culture* model, the determination to *cultivate a savvy sensitivity to the outside world.* This principle depends on the fact that *TO* employees see how their work connects to the organization's broad strategic intent. And they know that their opinions and knowledge are valued, not because their leaders say so, but because they are actually empowered to make decisions.

People in Thriving Organizations know their customers —the people who pay for their products and services. They pay attention to those people. They listen to them. And they make sure that what they learn in the process gets distributed throughout the organization.

Gore, Menlo Innovations, and CHG Healthcare all go to great lengths to understand in a deep way who their customers are and what they want and need. To develop this kind of savvy, they use a variety of unique practices to get close to them and stay close to them. (Again, we'll take a close look at some of these practices in the case study section.)

And being savvy isn't limited to customers. People across the enterprise in Thriving Organizations build similarly intimate relationships with their suppliers, who, in turn, provide them with market intelligence they'd never get otherwise. Through their customers and suppliers, they keep an eye out for competitors, making the organization much less vulnerable to being blindsided by some unforeseen disruption in the market. And they talk to people outside the organization about emerging technologies, changing economic conditions, relevant government activities—about anything and everything that can help them make better informed decisions.

They do all this not because they're forced, or even paid to do it. They do it because they want the organization to succeed, they feel as if they have a role to play in making that happen, and they know that the information they need to play that role is as likely to be found "out there" as it is internally.

So, when employees in a Thriving Organization pick up a bit of information from a customer or a supplier or a regulatory agency, they begin with the presumption that there might be something useful in what they've just learned. And they're likely to share it with someone else inside the organization to consider whether this is something the organization should act on, file away for future reference, or dismiss.

This is all less likely to happen in traditional hierarchical organizations because the decision makers are so far removed from the frontline employees that those employees don't believe that they will be heard if they say something. So they don't say anything, and as a result, what might potentially be useful information all too often never makes it into the organization's consciousness. Over time, that makes the organization less knowledgeable, less responsive, less agile—and quite possibly, less successful.

I once had an interesting conversation with a plant manager in a large, well-respected telecommunications firm. He told me that back when he was a program manager for software development in this same company, he had a boss he couldn't stand, so he moved into sales. And in this new role, he said, "Every day, I would hear from customers that our products sucked. As a program manager, I never heard that. I always thought we were doing great. That experience in sales was so useful to me when I came back to a managerial position in software development. At this point I'm on the fourth level of leadership in a company with seven levels. I'm classic middle management. But I'm at the last level of the hierarchy that actually has a sense of how what I do affects the customer. Above me, it's just moving numbers around on Excel spreadsheets."

What that manager learned, almost by accident, is how important it is to cultivate a savvy sense of your organization's place in the world—a sense you can't get from staying in your office and playing with spreadsheets.

And this isn't just a matter of being sensitive to obviously work-related sources of information, like customers and suppliers. Because they have a clear understanding of their organization's larger strategy, its business model, and its financial drivers, employees in a Thriving Organization are more likely to connect all of that to what they see and experience in the world *outside* of work—in their homes, in the books they read and the interests they pursue, in the conversations they have with friends and family members (who may sometimes even work for a competitor). And having made that connection—and sometimes recognizing something out there as a potential threat to their organization or a potential opportunity—they're more likely to bring that insight into work and act on it.

That's bringing the outside in.

ENABLE COLLABORATIVE EMERGENCE

Collaboration is big these days. Every manager wants to be perceived as a collaborative leader. Every team is charged with being collaborative. Every organization seems to tout its "collaborative processes" or "collaborative culture" somewhere on its website. But what do we mean by collaboration?

Too often, we confuse collaboration with *communication* (the basic exchange of information); *cooperation* (the willingness to provide assistance, often in the form of information or knowledge); or *coordination* (when the interdependencies between people and their actions are tight, and everyone does their part at exactly the right moment). Don't get me wrong: communication, cooperation, and coordination are all important to the success of a group, but I think collaboration goes further.

What distinguishes collaboration is synergy. Real collaboration involves a group of people working together in such a close and even intimate way that somehow, almost magically it seems, they reach a higher level of *collective* creativity. True collaboration enables the group to come up with something new or different, something they could not otherwise have discovered. In that sense, true collaboration almost always results in a surprise. In our model of the *TO Culture*, the term "collaborative emergence" speaks to this idea that true collaboration allows new ideas to emerge, out of the blue as it were.

Collaboration is enhanced when people bring diverse perspectives to bear on a given problem, especially when it's a wicked problem where there is no one right solution. In some organizations, differences in perspective often lead to conflict that prevents effective problem solving. But in a Thriving Organization, the culture's core axioms—to treat every member with respect, for example, and to focus on the common good—help ensure that these differences lead instead to creative tension and synergy.

Besides ensuring and embracing a variety of perspectives, organizations can enable collaborative emergence by making information readily and widely accessible. At Gore, the "lattice" structure of the organization was specifically intended to enable this easy, uninhibited flow of information. At Menlo Innovations and CHG Healthcare, the physical configuration of the workspace is designed to facilitate this information flow. Whatever it takes.

To enable collaborative emergence, the organization also needs to embrace uncertainty. There's a tendency, based on the traditional hierarchical model, to think that one of management's most important tasks is to remove uncertainty, as though the average employee can't be expected to make a good decision on their own in situations where absolutely everything is not spelled out. That's because uncertainty introduces variability into processes, and the traditional organization wants to minimize variability and maximize consistency and predictability. That's why so many organizations try to lay down rules to cover almost every situation that might arise. That's why their job descriptions are often ridiculously over-specified, and their policy manuals are impenetrably thick. No uncertainty here!

But what happens when uncertainty does rear its ugly head in an organization with this mindset? What happens when something comes up, and people aren't clear how the existing rules and processes apply? Faced with those situations, some people will get creative. They'll look for some way to work around the existing rules and processes, so they can solve the problem and move forward. But I suspect that more often, people in that situation try to keep their head down, hoping that the problem either goes away or gets handled by someone else.

By contrast, in a Thriving Organization, the rules are kept simple, to give people as much flexibility as possible in responding to new and unexpected challenges. In a Thriving Organization, uncertainty is seen not so much, or at least not only, as a threat. It's also seen as a challenge, an opportunity, a stimulus to innovation, a powerful force that pushes a group of people to work together more closely. Uncertainty creates a kind of positive stress that somehow stimulates a group to unleash creativity its members would never tap into otherwise.

Here's an interesting example of how collaborative emergence can create surprises. A well-known provider of corporate travel services is organized so that each corporate client is served by its own dedicated team of travel professionals. The mission of each team is to follow the client's travel policies, deliver timely service, minimize travel costs, and maximize the traveler experience. These teams are geographically distributed to better serve their clients, many of whom are global companies. But all members of a given team report to a common supervisor, and they have all been trained in specifically how to respond to the situations they typically encounter.

But what happens when a client calls with an unusual set of circumstances, a situation that falls outside of the team member's knowledge or is genuinely unscripted? In the past, the team member would say, "Do you mind if I get back to you while I escalate this to my supervisor?" But often, the supervisor —who typically has not been in the trenches for some time—needed to consult with other members of the leadership team or with the client to decide on a course of action. Obviously, this took time, and since most of the leaders are similarly far removed from day-to-day travel issues, the solution they came up with frequently turned out not to be the best one possible.

To see if there might be a better way of handling these uncertain situations, the company tried an experiment. They did away with the supervisors! They gave the members of each team access to a common online chat room. They also created team, rather than individual, performance metrics that triggered performance bonuses.

What resulted was collaborative emergence. Now when a team member wasn't sure what to do in a particular situation, they could send a chat message to the other members of their team—and someone almost always had a relevant experience or could suggest an innovative response. And they'd get back to the person with the question almost immediately! No time lost while the question got escalated. No "out-of-date, out-of-touch" solutions.

The result? Customer satisfaction scores went up significantly. And equally significant, the engagement scores of the travel professionals went up because they now felt greater ownership of the overall service delivered to their customers. That's what can happen when you enable collaborative emergence.

I find this anecdote interesting for several reasons. As I said, the original organizational structure for this group was the traditional hierarchical bureaucracy, with 20 or so workers reporting to one supervisor. The workers all had their job descriptions, their KPIs, their bonuses determined by their independent performance. And yet, when collaboration was enabled, performance went up. *What was thought to be independent performance actually wasn't.*

The point is that even when it appears that people are working independently, collaborating enables them to learn from each other, and in the process improve both their own and the group's performance.

Another point here. People—and this seems to be especially true for today's young people—generally like to work together. Even if they're introverts, most people seem to thrive on the social contact that collaboration entails. As human beings, we are, after all, social creatures. The travel advisors in the above example were still primarily working independently, but even the small amount of purposeful collaboration that the chat room enabled had significant payoffs, in terms of both employee engagement and customer satisfaction.

INVEST IN FUTURE CAPACITY

Starting back in the 1980s, many publicly traded companies bought into the idea that their primary, indeed, their only, obligation was to "maximize shareholder value." This idea, articulated by the Nobel Prize–winning economist Milton Friedman and championed at the time by celebrity CEOs like GE's Jack Welch, became so embedded in the management litany that it was eventually adopted and adapted by many privately held organizations.[7]

At about the same time that maximizing shareholder value was taking hold, the stock market was increasingly coming to be dominated by large institutions who placed their portfolios in the hands of professional investment managers, whose focus tended to be decidedly more short-term than the individual investors who had previously dominated the market. (As recently as the 1960s, stocks were held for eight years on average; today, most stocks in the U.S. are held

---

7   It's worth noting that Welch has since changed his mind. In 2009, he called maximizing shareholder value the "dumbest idea in the world" and went on to say that "... shareholder value is a result, not a strategy ... your main constituencies are your employees, your customers and your products."

less than a year, and perhaps as briefly as four months.) [8] As a result, over time, the concept came to mean maximize *short-term* shareholder value—and for the leaders of publicly held enterprises, that basically meant doing whatever was necessary to meet or exceed Wall Street's expectations for this quarter.

It comes down to whether you put your money on "exploiting our existing strengths" or "investing in what we might become." In companies where one of the core principles is *maximize (short-term) shareholder value*, that choice almost always resolves itself in favor of exploiting current strengths—continuing to "do what we do best."

The problem, of course, is that this kind of thinking doesn't do much to prepare the organization for that unseen competitor lurking out there with a disruptive technology. Kodak famously kept betting that people would always want to shoot film, that they'd keep stocking up on Kodak's iconic little yellow boxes rather than turn to those new-fangled digital cameras. And the irony is that Kodak could have been a player in the new world of digital technology if they'd invested in the future and not the past.

In Thriving Organizations, however, the underlying assumption is that the company's long-term success depends on its continuing to invest in future capacity. At Gore, for example, this principle is explicitly stated in these terms: "We believe in the long-term view. Our decisions are based on long-term payoff, and we don't sacrifice our fundamental beliefs at Gore for short-term gain[8]." In practice, this manifests itself in the fact that the time-to-profit for many Gore businesses has been far longer than a company with a short-term focus would have tolerated.

Here's another important point. In a Thriving Organization, the principle of investing in future capacity is intimately related to the very

---

8   See http://www.politifact.com/virginia/statements/2016/jul/06/mark-warner/mark-warner-says-average-holding-time-stocks-has-f/ .

definition of a *TO*—namely, that such an organization enables its people to thrive. In a company driven by the principle of maximizing short-term shareholder value, money might well be invested in training a machine operator to learn how to operate a new machine, because the short-term ROI is clear. At a company like Gore, however, investing in future capacity would also allow the company to invest in that machine operator's learning graphic design, even though the short-term ROI is impossible to measure. Why? Because this would help the Associate find what Gore refers to as a new "sweet spot," and by doing so, help the Associate thrive—which would in turn help the organization thrive.

And take the example of TD Industries, a 2,500-person, employee-owned construction company that has been on the 100 Best Companies to Work For list for the last 20 years. They support 32 hours of training for every employee every year, and the training choice is completely up to the employee, whether the focus is on professional or personal development. TDI itself offers hundreds of training programs internally. But if an employee wants to take an external program that's not offered internally, the company will cover 100 percent of the costs. That's investing in future capacity!

Remember our earlier discussion of tame problems vs. wicked problems? A company that's focused on continuing to do what it does best will tend to focus on tame problems, the kind that lend themselves to analysis and the application of generally accepted algorithms. And its investment in future capacity will mirror those tendencies. So, yes, such an organization will invest in a leadership development program, but that program will be focused primarily on ensuring that there will be a pool of leaders available to replace those expected to leave—a pool of leaders trained to do things pretty much the same way that those previous leaders have done things. Similarly, such a company's R&D investment is likely to be focused mostly on so-called incremental innovation—extensions and enhancements of existing products.

So, yes, these companies are investing in future capacity—but that investment is based on an underlying (and perhaps, unconscious) assumption that the future is relatively predictable.

Thriving Organizations view the future differently. They recognize and to some extent, embrace the fact that they live in a VUCA world, where the real challenge is to solve wicked, rather than tame, problems. With that in mind, they invest in future *adaptive* capability. Recognizing that they can't be sure *what* they will need for the future, they make bets on a variety of alternatives in the hope of giving themselves—as individuals and as an organization—enough options to meet whatever challenges and capture whatever opportunities the future presents

EXPECT LEADERSHIP EVERYWHERE

As we've already seen, the traditional hierarchical model was designed to place decision making squarely in the hands of a few top leaders. They were—supposedly—the smartest, the best informed, and the most disciplined guys (virtually always guys) in the room. It was inconceivable that anyone else would be trusted to keep the company on track for success.

But as we've also seen, things are different in a Thriving Organization. If one of the *TO's* basic axioms is that decisions should be made at the lowest level, and if one of the values-in-use is self-responsibility, it follows that one of the principles in the *TO Culture* would have to be *expect leadership everywhere*.

Whatever different structures and practices they employ, Thriving Organizations practice some form of distributed leadership. In a January 2017 interview, Professor Deborah Ancona of the MIT Sloan School of Management discussed her research into distributed leadership. She noted that:

The person at the top of an organization can no longer—not that they ever really could—deal with the complex issues of our time. And so, how do you set up a system that collectively creates entrepreneurial leaders [across the organization] who are leading change efforts? Leadership is not just about the person. It's about a collective of folks who are coming together to make new things and make things happen.[xi]

In his book, *Joy, Inc.*, Rich Sheridan says that "Leadership at Menlo does not rest with a title or a position. Some leadership is situational. Some leadership grows through increasing influence based on respect and experience."[xii] At Gore, this same principle is expressed variously as, "There are no traditional hierarchies at Gore, but we're not a completely flat organization," and, "Leaders [at Gore] most often emerge based on skill, capability and followership—or their potential to build followership over time."

Again, different Thriving Organizations may look quite different in terms of their leadership model. CHG, for example, looks more hierarchical than Gore or Menlo Innovations. But in order to truly thrive as we've defined the term, all Thriving Organizations look for, expect, encourage, and empower leadership to spring up all over the organization.

In Thriving Organizations, the concept of leadership tends to be quite broad. Some leaders help teams succeed. Some are champions of new initiatives. Some rely on unique technical or business expertise. Some are "meta-structurers," Deborah Ancona's term for leaders who focus on creating the organizational architecture and environment that allows the culture and organization members to thrive.

Because leadership in a Thriving Organization is not so much a function of position but of capacity to contribute what's needed to move a project, a team, or a business along at any given moment, leadership is very fluid. Now this person is leading, now that person is leading. In Thriving Organizations, even leaders with positional authority recognize the importance of knowing when to lead from the front, when to lead from behind, and when to step aside and let someone else lead.

And while Thriving Organizations may employ different leadership *structures* and employ different types of leadership, the leaders in those organizations do tend to share a set of attitudes and behaviors. The authors of *Firms of Endearment*, for example, note that the leaders of FoEs "are exemplars of what has come to be called 'servant leadership.'" They go on to quote one of these leaders, C. William Pollard, chairman of Servicemaster:

> *Servant leaders believe in the people they lead and are always ready to be surprised by their potential. Servant leaders make themselves available. Servant leaders are committed—they are not simply holders of position. They love and care for the people they lead.*[xiii]

Larry Spears, who has written extensively about servant leadership, lists these 10 characteristics of the servant leader: *listening, empathy, healing, awareness, persuasion, conceptualization, foresight, stewardship, commitment to the growth of people, and building community.*[xiv] It's not hard to see how these characteristics would fit well within a *TO Culture*.

Different from, but certainly not in conflict with, the characteristics of a servant leader identified by Spears, are the four leadership capabilities—*sensemaking, relating, visioning,* and *inventing*—laid out by MIT's Deborah Ancona in her article, "In Praise of the Incomplete Leader." As with Spears's framework, it's easy to see how Professor Ancona's four capabilities are well suited to Thriving Organizations.

Sensemaking requires a "savvy sensitivity to the outside world." It's about creating a coherent strategic narrative—gathering, absorbing, and synthesizing information, and seeing what is and is not important. It's about translating what can otherwise be a confusing and even overwhelming flood of data into a useful map of the operating environment.

Relating is about being able to see and connect with people in a real way. It's about empathy, about being compassionate. Visioning is about painting a compelling picture of the future—a picture with the power to pull people together around a common purpose. And finally, inventing is about making that vision of the future a reality, tapping the potential of the organization's people to create winning solutions to those wicked problems.

It's no wonder that it's hard, if not impossible, to find leaders who can do it all, which is why Thriving Organizations find ways to tap the leadership potential of people at every level. If every leader is necessarily "incomplete," then why not encourage more people to contribute to the organization's success? Why not expect—and enable—leadership everywhere?

Here's one last example of how this principle can make a huge difference in an organization's performance. In 1999, David Marquet took command of the USS *Santa Fe*, a nuclear-powered submarine in the Pacific fleet.[xv] It was the worst performing sub in the fleet. The crew members were frustrated, disengaged, looking to transfer, and looking to exit the Navy. And Marquet had only six months to get the ship ready for deployment, a very tight timeline.

Marquet had long believed that the Navy's command-and-control model was no longer appropriate in the complex, technical environment of nuclear submarines, where everyone's brains and commitment are necessary for success. He felt that the model essentially created a ship full of followers when a ship full of leaders was required.

Some 10 years earlier, as the engineering officer aboard another sub, Marquet had tried unsuccessfully to implement more of a distributed leadership model within his 60-person team. But he learned some important lessons in his failure. And so, faced with the seemingly impossible task of getting the *Santa Fe* ready in time, he was ready to try again.

One of the changes Marquet introduced was having the crew transition from "Request permission to . . ." to "I intend to." So, for example, "request permission to submerge" became "I intend to submerge." In addition, the crew member would state the reasoning behind the intended action, as in "I intend to submerge the ship. We are in water we own, water depth has been checked and is 400 feet, all men are below, the ship is rigged for dive, and I've certified my watch team."

With the explanation clearly stated, anyone within earshot who had contrary information was free to speak up, as in "We're only in 200 feet of water, not 400." In other cases, the intended action might be based on accurate information, but there might be unintended, unanticipated consequences. And again, with the explanation clearly stated, someone else—including but not limited to a senior officer—could step up to offer new, potentially important, information. As a result, the *Santa Fe*'s crew members began to develop a greater appreciation for the interconnectedness of all the ship's systems and processes, as well as a greater sense of responsibility for all aspects of its performance, not just their own, more limited area.

As the crew readied the ship for deployment, Marquet continued to institute practices that furthered the objective of creating a ship filled with leaders. He encouraged problem solving, rather than giving solutions. He put in place new measurement systems, designed to provide the crew with information that would allow them to learn. He promoted "deliberate action" rather than rote response, again, in ways that allowed people to reflect on, and learn from, their actions and the consequences of those actions.

The result? The *Santa Fe* met its six-month deployment deadline, and after one year, went from the worst-performing nuclear sub in the Pacific fleet to the best. And as for the crew, morale, retention, and re-enlistment rose significantly. All from expecting leadership everywhere.

By cultivating a savvy sensitivity to the outside world, enabling collaborative emergence, and expecting leadership everywhere, Thriving Organizations operate as what Peter Senge identified as "learning organizations."

In Senge's words, learning organizations are ". . . organizations where people continually expand their capacity to create the results they truly desire, where new and expansive patterns of thinking are nurtured, where collective aspiration is set free, and where people are continually learning to see the whole together."

THE *TO CULTURE:*
VALUES-IN-USE

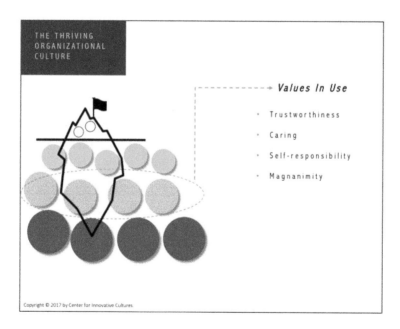

THE THRIVING
ORGANIZATIONAL
CULTURE

Values In Use

· Trustworthiness

· Caring

· Self-responsibility

· Magnanimity

Copyright © 2017 by Center for Innovative Cultures.

Over time, human beings, and by extension, the organizations they create, develop a set of values that are important to them, whether or not those values are consciously held and articulated. Some of these values will be more important than others. And while some (those we refer to as *values-in-use*) will significantly shape individual and organizational behavior, others may be more aspirational in nature.

In an organizational culture, the values-in-use flow out of the culture's basic assumptions about people and organizations, and, in turn, the values-in-use shape a set of principles that guide the organization's behavior and artifacts. In the last chapter, we discussed several critical principles at work in Thriving Organizations.

It's easy to lay out a fairly long list of values that manifest themselves in Thriving Organizations. Some of these will differ from one Thriving Organization to another because those particular values are related to that particular organization's unique strategic intent and operational requirements.

For example, W.L. Gore has built its success over these past six decades by inventing a steady flow of new products derived from polytetrafluorethylene, a chemical compound originally developed by DuPont and commercially known as TEFLON®. Not surprisingly, then, *innovation* is an important value-in-use at Gore. By contrast, innovation is not one of the values-in-use at CHG Healthcare, whose success is not based on inventing anything new. CHG would say that building *close relationships with clients and providers* is one of their key values-in-use because it is critical to their strategic intent of customer intimacy.

For the purposes of our model, we've elected not to include values that are in this sense related to the organization's strategic intent. Rather, the four we've chosen—*trustworthiness, caring, self-responsibility,* and *magnanimity*—are part of the deep dynamics of all *TO Cultures*, regardless of the specific strategic intent and operational requirements of the particular organization. Let's see how.

TRUSTWORTHINESS

Nearly everyone agrees that high-performing organizations manifest a high degree of trust. Conversely, many dysfunctional organizations manifest a high degree of *distrust*. Trust and distrust, however, are not in themselves values. Rather, they are outcomes—the result of the countless decisions and actions of individuals within the organization. You get trust when those decisions and actions demonstrate that the individuals can be trusted to do the right thing. You get trust when people, and the organization they constitute, prove themselves to be trustworthy.

Trustworthiness means following through on commitments and doing what one says one is going to do. It also implies honesty and integrity and acting ethically. If I say I'm going to rob a bank, and I rob a bank, I've done what I said I was going to do, but would I be considered trustworthy? Hardly.

Trustworthiness flows from a fairly accurate sense of one's own abilities, capabilities, and contributions. People often try to do things beyond their level of competence. That's a good thing. It means they are stretching and trying to grow. But to really be considered trustworthy, you must be able to deliver, at least more often than not. And equally importantly, you need to acknowledge what you are *not* capable of. No one trusts someone who claims to be capable of great feats outside their area of expertise who can't deliver.

The honesty and integrity aspects of trustworthiness come into play when we fail to deliver on a commitment we've made. In that case, making excuses or blaming others for our failure will mark us as anything *but* trustworthy. Similarly, if we exaggerate our contribution or take credit for something others actually accomplished, this will again mark us as not being trustworthy.

What about organizations? What marks them as trustworthy or untrustworthy? One thing is certain: saying it doesn't make it so. It's hard to imagine an organization—and again, we're really talking about the organization's leaders here—that doesn't say that it values trust, and by implication, trustworthiness. But to actually be trustworthy, an individual must make a commitment and then stick to it—and in far too many organizations, employees are not *allowed* to make a commitment. Rather, they are told what to do, and they're expected to obey—which is different from making a self-declared commitment. In effect, the organization denies its employees the opportunity to prove themselves truly trustworthy.

The organization does the same thing by putting in place rules and policies that demonstrate that it doesn't consider its employees trustworthy. One small, but I think quite interesting, story in this regard comes out of my time at Gore. Over the years, as the company expanded globally, travel costs increased significantly. Like other companies, Gore had to decide how to manage these expenses.

Unlike so many other companies, however, Gore decided that its people could be trusted to make the right decisions in this regard, without a lot of rules. As a result, Gore's travel policy came down to a couple of paragraphs that basically said: spend the company's money as if it were your own. The closest thing to a real rule was that for international travel, Gore Associates generally were expected to fly coach, but for trips of nine hours or more, they could decide whether to fly business class. That's it: two paragraphs.

At one point, a Gore Associate passed along a conversation he had had with a representative of the large global travel agency that arranged all of Gore's overseas travel. The travel rep had explained that unlike Gore, most companies had pages of rules covering travel expenses. But to his surprise, his company's statistics showed that Gore Associates spent *less* on various travel expenses than employees in these other companies. It appeared that lots of travel rules and detailed travel policies invited "gaming the system." By contrast, Gore in effect proved that it valued trustworthiness by treating its people as if they were, in fact, trustworthy.

CARING

The Gallup Organization has probably studied employee engagement more extensively than anyone else. Much of their research is based on their proprietary Q12 survey instrument, which tests how employees rate their company on a variety of engagement-related metrics—one of which is *My supervisor, or someone at work, seems to care about me as a person.* As it turns out, this sense that "the organization cares about me" is critical to whether an employee is likely to be engaged or disengaged.

There is also a considerable body of academic research into various aspects of caring. Sigal Barsade and Mandy O'Neill have studied "companionate love." Monica Worline and Jane Dutton have studied "compassion." My colleague at Westminster, Vicki Whiting, has studied "kindness." Different as the perspectives may be, as a whole, this work speaks to the fact that we all want others to care about us, and we all derive deep satisfaction from caring for others. In other words, we value caring—in our personal life, in our family life, in our organizational life.

But does it really make sense to talk about caring in an organizational context? Yes, my supervisor may seem to care about me, but can my *organization* care about me? And if it can, why would it? After all, the organization—at least if it's a business—is interested first and foremost in making money. And if for some reason, the organization may truly be said to value caring, how will this manifest itself?

For many traditional organizations, caring is simply not a value-in-use, and, in fact, it may not even be an espoused or aspirational value. If the object of the game is to maximize employee output to maximize profits and/or shareholder value, it's easy to conclude, consciously or otherwise, that caring about the organization's employees isn't as important as making sure that they do what they're supposed to do. It's easy to start thinking of those employees as resources to be managed, rather than as individual human beings who deserve to be treated in a caring manner. That way, it's easier to lay them off, or cut their benefits, or subject them to a high-stress work environment, if that's what it takes to make the numbers work.

Caring, after all, requires an organization to recognize that even at work, people are human and that sometimes, life gets in the way of performance. Kids get sick. Parents get old. Marriages fall apart. Is it realistic to expect that people won't bring this life-stuff into work? When they do, how should the organization respond?

But caring isn't only about helping people get through tough times. It's also about celebrating who they are as unique individuals. It's about recognizing what they bring to the organization, in ways that may include but also go beyond the objectives they meet or the numbers they deliver. It's about seeing their potential, investing in them, supporting them, and giving them the honest feedback they need to become their best selves.

Let me hit that last point a bit harder. In many organizations, and, indeed, in many interpersonal relationships, giving someone "honest feedback" may be couched in terms of helping the other person improve, but often it's about scoring points, or taking the other person down a notch. That has nothing to do with caring, nothing to do with wanting to create the conditions in which the other person can thrive.

You might be thinking, "That's all pretty soft stuff. It might be nice, but what does it have to do with the business of being a business?"

I think the answer is simple. Employees who feel that their organization truly cares about them are more likely to make a commitment to its success. They're less likely to jump ship, and more likely to be highly engaged, to put in that extra effort that can make the difference between good and great results. In other words, by caring about its people, the organization helps them thrive, which, in turn, helps the organization itself thrive.

That's what happened when Gore and CHG made the decision not to implement significant layoffs when the economy went south in 2008. That's what happens when CHG's leaders turn the lights off at the office at six o'clock every night, to ensure that their employees have time for a life outside of work. It's what happens when Gore encourages Associates to find their sweet spot, a role that not only meets the company's needs but also maps closely to the Associate's interests and capabilities—even if these need to be developed. It's what happens when Menlo Innovations allows new moms to bring their newborn babies to work when they're still too young for day care.

SELF-RESPONSIBILITY

Let's talk about what it means to be responsible. When we talk about a person's being responsible *for* something, we're essentially referring to their role. There's no particular value attached to that use of the word. So, we might say Bill is responsible for logging the miles on company vehicles and scheduling routine maintenance. But when we say that Joe or Janice is a responsible *person*, we mean that they are reliable; they can be counted on. And *that* has value.

In this sense, "responsible" sounds a lot like "trustworthy," and it has a high value to command and control leaders, whose role is to decide what needs to be done and how it should be done. Leaders operating in this mode expect (demand?) that their employees will be responsible and do what they're supposed to do.

Thriving Organizations take things up a notch by placing a high value not just or not so much on responsibility, but on *self-responsibility*. Self-responsibility goes beyond compliance to ownership. The self-responsible individual doesn't just follow the rules and designated procedures laid down by the boss. The self-responsible person understands and is committed to doing the job right, and when the usual procedures can't handle a given situation, he or she actively looks for a better solution.

From the Netflix website, on the company's Culture of Freedom & Responsibility:

"There are companies where people walk by trash on the floor in the office, leaving it for someone else to pick it up, and there are companies where people lean down to pick up the trash they see, as they would at home. We try hard to be the latter, a company where everyone feels a sense of responsibility to do the right thing, to help the company at every juncture. Picking up the trash is the metaphor for taking care of problems, small and large, as you see them, and never thinking "that's not my job." We don't have rules about picking up the real or metaphoric trash. We try to create the sense of ownership, responsibility and initiative so that this behavior comes naturally."

As I was working on this book, a media uproar occurred over an incident in which United Airlines employees called airport security personnel to remove a passenger from his seat on a plane just before takeoff. The 67-year-old doctor was one of four passengers "randomly selected" to give up their seats to make room for other United crew members headed from Chicago to Louisville to staff another flight.

When he refused, the officers forcibly removed him, and he ended up with a concussion, a broken nose, and two lost teeth.

It turned out that the United employees had, in the CEO's words, "followed established procedures." They had, for example, first offered a $400 voucher for future travel to entice volunteers and then raised the amount to $800. Only then did they go to the random selection process (although it's worth noting that first-class passengers were not included). And only after they had failed to convince the doctor to leave his seat (the three other selected passengers complied) did they call security. In other words, the United employees in question acted responsibly.

What might self-responsibility have entailed in this situation? They could have upped the ante to secure volunteers. In the aftermath of the incident, United enacted a new set of procedures, including allowing compensation of up to $10,000 for similar situations. They could also have considered loading the four United crew members into a limo for the five-hour drive from Chicago to Louisville.

In order to exercise self-responsibility, employees (including line supervisors) need to understand the big picture—in this case, that their first responsibility is to make every passenger, as much as possible, feel safe and well cared for—and own their own role in that picture. They need to feel free—and empowered—to make decisions on their own in carrying out that role to the best of their ability.

Thriving Organizations value self-responsibility, and they enable it, by allowing employees the freedom to make meaningful decisions about how to do their jobs better, about how to develop their capabilities, about how to make the organization be more successful, and by giving feedback when an employee has not fully embraced "self-responsibility."

CHG's culture, for example, is built on the idea that employees can and should freely express their ideas and opinions about anything and everything that goes on at work. As one of its leaders put it:

> *Day 1, what they [the employees] hear is you own the culture. If it doesn't work for you, you have to change it to make it better. You can call it ownership or leadership, but what we would say is everyone owns the culture. Everyone is part of it. . . . [everyone has] a responsibility to better the culture from right now.*

At W.L. Gore, two of the company's four guiding principles are *freedom* and *commitment*. During my many years at Gore, I often heard Bill Gore expound on these principles, and he always linked the two. He would talk about how important it was for Associates to *feel* free and to *be* free to do their jobs in the right way. But he would always follow with something like, "But with freedom comes great responsibility . . ." and then he would do a riff on commitment and how one's commitments bounded one's freedom. He didn't use the term, but Bill was talking about self-responsibility.

I once commented to a colleague that when I talk to people about Gore and other companies where self-responsibility and self-management are considered important values, the response is frequently, "Yeah, but how do those companies hold people accountable when they don't perform?" My colleague replied, "I think they're asking the wrong question. It isn't about how you hold others accountable. It's about how you create an environment where people hold themselves accountable."

Encouraging all organizational members to exercise self-responsibility and make appropriate decisions on their own inevitably involves a degree of risk. After all, decisions don't always work out as planned, and so the organization must allow well-intentioned mistakes, so long as something is learned from the effort. The organization also needs to provide its members with guidelines that clarify what risks are okay for them to take, and what risks are too big to take.

One last example. The Other Side Academy in Salt Lake City is dedicated to changing the lives of people with a history of addiction and incarceration. I live and work in Salt Lake City, and I've spent some time with the folks at "TOSA," and I've always come away mightily impressed by their approach. There's little doubt in my mind that self-responsibility is a value-in-use at TOSA.

TOSA opened its doors in 2016. It now has over 50 "students." For those for whom TOSA is "alternative sentencing," each has convinced a judge to allow them to enroll in the program, with a minimum commitment of two years. The students live and work together: the students run TOSA's moving business and food truck.

There are no therapists or counselors at TOSA, no 12-step program. Most of the students have been through—and in the founder's words, "conned"—any number of such programs. At TOSA, they're told: "OK, you've had a tough life. And, yes, addiction is a disease. But the fact is that every time you take a drink, every time you shoot up, every time you commit a crime—you're making a free choice! We can help you learn to make better choices, but first, you have to understand that these choices are yours, and only yours. You need to own those choices."

In other words, it's about self-responsibility, which, by the way, includes not pointing fingers, making excuses, or passing the blame when things don't go the right way. Those are victim behaviors. People who are self-responsible always ask themselves if there was something they did that contributed to a less-than-desirable outcome. They don't beat themselves up about it. But they look at themselves first, or at least at the same time, as they look at others.

It's important to note that TOSA takes no government funding. One of their sayings is "There's no free lunch here. If you're eating, someone earned the money to buy the food." Again, it's about self-responsibility. And it's also important to note that the recidivism rate at TOSA is much better than at other kinds of treatment programs. They estimate that if you stay for two years, you have a 40 percent chance of staying clean. If you stay for three years, you have a 60 percent chance, and if you stay for four years, you have an 80 percent chance.

Encouraging, supporting, and enabling true self-responsibility—it's all critical to how Thriving Organizational cultures don't just allow you to bring your best self to work, but help you *become* your best self at work.

MAGNANIMITY

Magnanimity speaks to a generosity of spirit, a willingness to extend toward others an appreciation for their contribution to whatever success we (collectively) have achieved. In this sense, it's the opposite of the egocentric, credit-grabbing behavior that characterizes leaders who are more focused on their own personal success—and heaven forbid, their own personal brand—than on the success of the organization. That kind of behavior and the internal politics it generates almost inevitably prevent an organization from thriving. And it's not just business organizations. In the sports world, team chemistry is critical to success, and the "focus on my own stats" mentality of a self-aggrandizing superstar more often than not leads to failure.

Organizations that value magnanimity go to great lengths to celebrate teams and their achievements. Gore, CHG, and Menlo Innovations, for example, are all structured around small teams, and conversations with team members at any of these companies tend to evoke "We did this" much more than "I did this." In my own experience at Gore, I can say that leaders who were too concerned with drawing attention to themselves ultimately lost their "followership" and with it, their opportunities for continued leadership. At Menlo, everyone—including the CEO—works in the company's large, open workspace, a constant reminder that everyone contributes to the organization's success.

But magnanimity is more than just sharing credit. It includes a genuine appreciation for the complementary skills and talents that each individual brings to the collective success. In my experience at Gore, the recognition and appreciation of the success of others was clearly linked to a sense that "When one of us succeeds, we all succeed."

Abraham Maslow wrote about the necessity of what he called "the ability to admire" in thriving organizations. Organizations in which people lacked this appreciation of the unique talents and contributions of others tended to foster the sense of a zero-sum game: "I could have done that if I had the chance." "I was just as deserving of the promotion as she was."

Conversely, in organizations where this ability to admire is embedded in the culture, you're more likely to hear statements like, "You're the only person who could have pulled that off" and "Your ability to do x-y-z was crucial to our team's success." In this connection, it's interesting to refer again to Gallup's engagement research, which includes "recognition for my work" as one of the key drivers of employee engagement.

Before moving on, I'd like to touch on another connotation of magnanimity; namely, the sense that not only are we all in this together—that we all have something important to contribute—but that "together, we can do great things." The popular literature on leadership and organizational culture these days is replete with the importance of creating a sense of higher purpose. But if true magnanimity does not exist among an organization's members—and especially between leaders and followers—then the higher purpose, whatever it is said to be, is fated to be just another piece of empty rhetoric.

SYNERGY OF VALUES

As important as they are to the culture of Thriving Organizations, these four values-in-use also create some additional values in combination with one another. So, for example, when you combine trustworthiness with caring, you get *fairness*. Fairness doesn't mean that everyone is treated the same. Rather, it is an attempt to take into consideration the unique needs and circumstances in any situation and as much as possible, to devise a win-win situation. At Gore, fairness was always seen as multifaceted. What was fair to the Associate? What was fair to the team? What was fair to the enterprise? What was fair to the customer or supplier? Fairness required a look at all the stakeholders, and it always involved a judgment and not a policy.

When you combine caring with self-responsibility, you get what The Other Side Academy calls "200 percent accountability." This is a recognition that the members of the organization are fully accountable not only for themselves but also for all the other members with whom they come in contact. This value-in-use recognizes that it is not "caring" to let someone not do their best or to overlook violations of the norms and practices of the organization.

The point is there's nothing soft about Thriving Organizations and their values. Thriving Organizations can and should be very tough-minded in setting a high bar and challenging their people to be their best selves.

When you combine self-responsibility with magnanimity, you get *humble charisma*—what Jim Collins refers to in his discussion of Level 5 leadership. In organizations where this is a value-in-use, leaders transmit a compelling vision of what the organization can achieve, without making the journey about themselves. Where humble charisma is at work, leaders are clear that they can't make this journey on their own: they encourage—and empower—others to make their contribution to the effort.

So now let's get to the bottom of the iceberg. Let's examine the set of core *axioms* that ultimately generate all the other components of the *TO Culture*.

THE *TO CULTURE*: AXIOMS

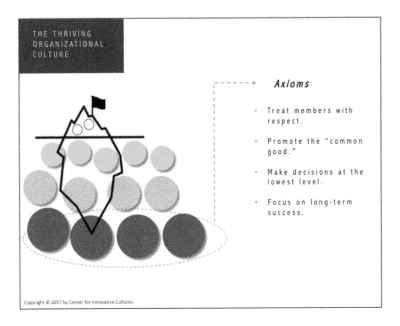

In organizations that thrive and enable their people to thrive, these four axioms are foundational:

- Treat the organization's members with the respect that human dignity demands.
- Promote the common good in making decisions and conducting business activities.

- Make decisions at the lowest possible level of the organization.
- Focus on long-term success.

Let's look at each of these axioms in greater detail.

TREAT MEMBERS WITH RESPECT

In a Thriving Organization, it is axiomatic that every member of the organization, regardless of role, has an inherent dignity, simply by virtue of their being human. That inherent dignity entitles them to be treated with respect. It means they are entitled to be treated courteously, entitled to have their ideas heard and seriously considered, not *as if* but *because* they and their ideas do indeed matter. It means they are entitled to significant autonomy and control over how they spend their time and do their work. They are entitled to be involved in some real way in the organization's decision-making process.

At W.L. Gore, for example, the company's statement of fundamental beliefs begins with, "We believe in the *individual* and each Associate's potential to help Gore grow and succeed." This deep-seated belief in the importance and value of each individual goes back to Bill Gore, the company's founder, who said:

> *I dreamed of an enterprise with great opportunity for all who would join in it, a virile organization that would foster self-fulfillment and which would multiply the capabilities of the individuals comprising it beyond their mere sum.*

This belief played itself out in many ways. Leaders at Gore, for example, were identified by the fact of their having followers—and every Gore leader was expected to earn and maintain followership from those they lead. Any Gore leader who consistently treated his/her team members in a disrespectful or untrustworthy manner would soon be a non-leader. In my experience, the kind of intimidation and bullying that routinely occurs in so many other organizations is rarely heard of at Gore.

The inherent dignity of the individual was also manifest at Gore in the fact that Associates felt free to express their ideas on matters large and small, knowing that those ideas would be treated with the respect they deserved. Note that "the respect they deserved" means that those ideas would also be challenged, often in a very spirited fashion, by Associates who disagreed, which is itself a form of real respect.

Unfortunately, far too many organizations fail to accord their employees this day-to-day respect. As one author notes:

> *In survey after survey, the biggest employee complaint is being treated with a lack of respect. Whether they work in an Amazon warehouse, serve fast food, or sit in .a customer service cubicle, they feel diminished by how they are treated.*[xvi]

PROMOTE THE COMMON GOOD

In a Thriving Organization, it is also axiomatic that the organization should act in the interests of all, and not just some, of its members. The authors of *Firms of Endearment* put it this way: "FoEs take an expansive worldview. They believe deeply in the possibility of a rising tide that raises all boats." W.L. Gore, also making use of a nautical metaphor, affirms that:

> *We also believe we're all in the same boat. As Associates, we have a vested interest in the success of the company, and we share in Gore's risks and rewards while having an added incentive to stay committed to our enterprise's long-term success. As a result, we feel we're all in this effort together, and believe we should always consider what's best for the enterprise as a whole when making decisions.*

At both Gore and CHG Healthcare, the commitment to the common good came into play when the financial crisis of 2008 began. Leaders in both companies were well aware that their competitors were responding to the economic downturn by drastically reducing their workforces. Both companies rejected that approach, working actively with their employees to come up with an array of cost-reduction strategies that enabled them to weather the crisis with only a very minimal reduction in force.

As with the fundamental belief that all members of an organization should be treated with respect, this commitment to the common good may receive lip service in many enterprises, but it is all too often ignored in practice. Particularly in corporate entities beholden to outside investors, the prevailing axiom, at least for the past three or more decades, has been that the organization's sole purpose is to maximize shareholder value. While this idea has lost some of its luster, it still holds sway in many executive suites, including many that are decidedly not thriving.

Let's leave aside the issue of whether an organization—and more specifically, a business organization—has any moral obligation to behave in ways that advance the interests of its employees, its customers, its suppliers, and the communities in which it operates, as well as its owners/investors. There's the question of whether it's even possible to do so. After all, won't the interests of the shareholders often conflict with those of those other stakeholders?

Based on their research, the authors of *Firms of Endearment* argue that the "shareholder versus stakeholder debate presents a false dichotomy." Using the example of companies like Costco, they maintain that: "Judging by the superior financial performance achieved by the exemplary companies cited in this book, we believe that the best way to create value for shareholders in the long run is by consciously creating value for all stakeholders."[xvii]

In further explanation, they quote Costco's former CEO as saying that paying rock-bottom wages [in the interests of maximizing short-term profits and thus the stock price] ". . . doesn't pay the right dividends. It doesn't keep employees happy. It keeps them looking for other jobs. Plus, managers spend all their time hiring replacements rather than running your business. We would rather have our employees running our business."

The operational problem with a single-minded focus on maximizing shareholder value is that it leads companies to focus too much on the short term, which, in turn, can lead to behavior that creates significant problems down the road. Whether it's layoffs that ultimately cost the company its best workers, cutting corners in the manufacturing process that eventually causes brand-damaging quality issues, or pressure to make the quarterly numbers that encourages a company's sales force to "stuff the pipeline" by incentivizing customers to order products at unsupportable prices—there's good reason to agree with Jack Welch, once a leading proponent of maximizing shareholder value, who now calls it "the dumbest idea in the world."

MAKE DECISIONS AT THE LOWEST LEVEL

If you honestly believe that all the members of your organization should be treated with respect—if you believe that they are capable individuals and their ideas are critical to the organization's success—it follows that you will want to engage those people and their ideas in the organization's decision-making process. With that in mind, it is axiomatic in the Thriving Organization that decisions should be made at the lowest level possible in the organization, which means that in many cases, small teams and individual employees will have the autonomy to make many decisions on their own. It also means that even decisions which more appropriately should be made at the enterprise level will in a Thriving Organization draw explicitly on input from those working at lower levels.

That's not the way it works in many organizations, where key decisions get made by leaders at the top, with little real participation from those at lower levels. And what happens in these organizations when issues arise at those lower levels? Not surprisingly, the people directly confronting the issue, often the people with the most direct knowledge of how to resolve it, typically kick the decision upstairs. This is likely to have the dual effect of making the organization less agile and responsive while making the people in the organization feel less respected and therefore making them less engaged.

By contrast, the authors of *Firms of Endearment* note that "FoE employees generally have the authority (and the obligation) to spend the resources to make a customer happy or fix a production problem."[xviii] And at Gore, the company's lattice structure was specifically designed to push decision making down to the lowest appropriate level and facilitate the flow of information across the enterprise rather than just from the top down. Gore relies heavily on small teams, which have considerable decision-making autonomy, and Gore plants are kept small (typically only a few hundred Associates) to further encourage local decision making. Individual Associates are similarly encouraged and indeed expected to make appropriate decisions on their own, although it is also expected that they will seek input from others as necessary, especially on issues that could have a significant impact on the Enterprise. And on a day-to-day basis, when Gore Associates need information to solve a problem, they go directly to the person who has that information, rather than passing a request to their leader who will, in turn, pass it to another leader.

FOCUS ON LONG-TERM SUCCESS

Closely tied to the Thriving Organization's commitment to the common good is a focus on long-term success. In W.L. Gore's terms:

> *Finally, we believe in the long-term view. Our decisions are based on long-term payoff, and we don't sacrifice our fundamental beliefs at Gore for short-term gain.*

Commenting on this same mindset, the authors of *Firms of Endearment* note that:

> *Google's founders, for example, have clearly stated that they believe "shareholders are better off in the long run when the company is doing good things for the world even though they might have to let go of some profits in the short run."*

As we have seen, this commitment to long-term success means that Thriving Organizations like Gore and CHG can react to hard times by saying: "Yes, we could cut costs and sustain profitability for now by cutting our workforce, but by retaining those loyal, well-trained employees we'll be better positioned for success when the economy recovers."

This focus on long-term success also drives Thriving Organizations to stay relentlessly committed to delivering high-quality products and services that produce exceptional levels of customer satisfaction.

At Gore, the commitment to long-term success is intimately related to the company's passion for quality and customer satisfaction. For example, in the 1980s, when first-generation products made from the company's then new GORE-TEX® fabric did not perform as promised under extremely wet conditions, the company offered to buy back, from retailers *and their customers*, all the garments that had been sold using the faulty fabric.

One last point.

In discussing how the basic assumptions that underlie every organizational culture are formed, Schein argued that they develop through the experience of solving important problems:

> *When a solution to a problem works repeatedly, it comes to be taken for granted. What was once a hypothesis, supported only by a hunch or a value, gradually comes to be treated as reality.*

These assumptions, of course, reside in the minds of the people who make up the organization, most particularly the organization's leaders, and these people carry their assumptions with them when they move from one organization to another. But they only become foundational to a given culture when they are so widely accepted in that organization that, as Schein points out, "members will find behavior based on any other premise inconceivable." At that point, "they tend to be non-confrontable and non-debatable, and hence are extremely difficult to change."[xix]

But what happens when new problems that require new solutions confront the organization? As we've already seen, this is precisely the situation facing many, if not most, companies today, in the face of globalization, digitization, etc. In that case, it can be extremely difficult to develop those new solutions, since the organization is trying to do so on the basis of core assumptions that are no longer as useful as they once were—and which are non-confrontable and nondebatable.

So now, let's examine some strategies that can help an organization—that can help you—overcome this challenge of making significant changes to an existing organizational culture. Let's talk about how you go about building a *TO Culture*.

PART III
MOVING YOUR ORGANIZATION TOWARD A *TO CULTURE*

IT'S EASIER—BUT NOT EASY—
IF YOU START FROM SCRATCH

In new organizations, the founders begin to shape the culture right from Day One. If a founder is committed to building a Thriving Organization, the *TO Culture*, with its underlying axioms, values, and principles, can, in that sense, be embedded into the organization's DNA.

That was certainly true for W.L. Gore & Associates. In 1958, after 17 years as a research chemist at DuPont, Bill Gore, along with his wife Vieve, decided to launch their own company. They took the money from Bill's retirement fund, mortgaged their house, and set up shop in their basement. Bill had a deep understanding of DuPont's patented polytetrafluorethylene polymer—TEFLON®'s chemical name—and he had DuPont's blessing, and promise of support, to pursue a wire-and-cable product based on TEFLON® technology.

At DuPont, Bill had worked on several task forces—small, cross-functional teams that operated with considerable autonomy within the larger corporate structure. These task forces were typically formed when the traditional functional hierarchy was unable to solve a problem or come up with a way to take advantage of an opportunity. Bill had come away deeply impressed by how these small groups fostered an environment where everyone was highly engaged and fully committed to the work, how the team members thoroughly enjoyed themselves (and each other) while doing that work, and most of all, how effective the task forces were in solving tough, technical problems.

Bill was also impressed—sadly impressed—by how quickly the task force "high" would disappear when the members of the task force returned to their normal roles within the hierarchy. Ideas no longer came from anyone, but only the subject matter experts. And people didn't address one another by their first name. It was back to "Dr. So-and-So," "Mr./Mrs./Miss So-and-So." Bill was determined to create the task force environment in W.L. Gore & Associates. And he did so by, among other things, avoiding the functional hierarchy and instead, instilling the motto, "Organize around opportunity." What is it fundamentally that we are trying to accomplish? Who wants to do it? Okay, let's get to work.

In addition to DuPont's task forces, Bill's vision for Gore and Associates as it evolved was informed by Abraham Maslow's "Hierarchy of Needs," and Douglas McGregor's idea of Theory Y management. In a paper published in 1943 and later in his 1954 book, *Motivation and Personality*, Maslow argued that human beings are internally motivated to meet five basic needs: physiological, safety, belonging, esteem, and self-actualization. Some organizations might meet one or two of these needs, but self-actualization was rarely one of them.

McGregor, in his 1960 bestseller, *The Human Side of Enterprise*, built on Maslow's fundamentally positive view of human nature by contrasting two management models.

"Theory X" managers assume that most people are not, in fact, self-motivated and need to be driven to carry out the organization's required tasks. Management thought and practice has generally evolved from a "Mean" Theory X approach, where threats and punishments dominate, to a "Nice" Theory X approach, where rewards and incentives are meant to manipulate employees to do management's bidding. ("Nice" is nicer than "Mean," but it still subscribes to the same negative view of people at work.)

"Theory Y" leaders, on the other hand, assume that people are intrinsically motivated to develop their full potential, and that given greater opportunities for autonomy and self-direction, they will derive satisfaction from the work itself and will do that work with more energy, enthusiasm, and creativity than they could ever be compelled to apply.

And so, right from its inception and as it developed, Gore's culture was based on the idea that everyone in the organization had a crucial contribution to make to the company's success, and that they should, therefore, be treated with respect. In turn, that meant caring about their success, making sure that they had the opportunity to become their best selves, giving them as much autonomy as possible, and creating a structure in which decision making was widely dispersed.

I first became involved with W.L. Gore 25+ years after Bill launched the business, and I can attest to the fact that he was still passionate about creating a thriving culture. I can also vouch for the fact that over the next three decades, people at Gore remained equally passionate about preserving the essence of that culture while adapting it to the opportunities and challenges that global growth, increased competition, and new technological discoveries brought.

From a historical perspective, I might add that the word "culture" itself didn't enter the Gore vocabulary until well after the company was up and running. (Bill was fond of referring to his principles as the "philosophy of the Enterprise.") And I'm actually rather proud of the fact that on the "milestone wall" at the company's Capabilities Center in

Newark, NJ, a plaque at the 1985 mark reads: *In his personal memoir, Bill Gore credits Michael Pacanowsky, a communications professor on sabbatical at Gore, for first applying the term "culture" to the organization.*

And then there's Menlo Innovations. When Rich Sheridan launched Menlo with cofounder James Goebel in 2001, they knew that they wanted to create a company in which people would experience the special joy of creating outstanding products that consistently exceed the customer's expectations. Going even beyond that, their vision was to create a company that would help "end human suffering as it relates to technology." Wow!

From the beginning, they believed that every member of the organization should be treated with respect, that every member should have a voice in decision making. They were committed to the values and principles of a Thriving Organization: trustworthiness, caring, self-responsibility, magnanimity, connecting the dots, collaborative emergence, etc. And they were convinced, right from Day One, that building this kind of culture would be critical to the company's long-term success.

But just because the founder of an organization *intends* to build a *TO Culture*, that doesn't make it easy to do. For one thing, he or she has to bring others on board who share this vision—a challenge that will need to be faced again and again as the organization grows.

There are always choices to be made about practices and artifacts: what kind of organizational structure, processes, information flow, workspace, reward system, and so forth will enable the organization to thrive? Those choices must be based on the organization's strategic intent, industry, market, products and services, customers, and so on.

And those choices must *work* in order for the founder's values and assumptions to become embedded in the culture. As Schein points out:

Only if the resulting behavior leads to "success"—in the sense that the group accomplishes its task and the members feel good about their relationships to each other—will the founder's beliefs and values be confirmed and reinforced, and most important, come to be recognized as <u>shared</u>.[xx]

And, of course, there's also the issue of sustaining the culture in the face of the inevitable internal and external challenges the organization will confront over time. The organization's continued success and even its survival in the face of these challenges will depend on its ability to make appropriate changes to its culture.

During my time at Gore, most of my work had to do with the culture. I started and managed the annual culture survey, which gave everyone in the organization an opportunity to reflect on how well the culture was continuing to meet the needs of both the Enterprise and the Associates. The survey results were discussed throughout the organization, a conversation that one Gore leader told me is absolutely crucial because ". . . if we don't act as good stewards of the culture, we will wake up one morning and realize that it has evolved into something we just don't like. We just can't let that happen."

According to Terri Kelly, Gore's CEO from 2005 to 2018, the survey is crucial in this sense:

If the Enterprise is not performing, we may need to change the culture. But before we change the culture, we also need to know, are we practicing the culture the way it's supposed to be practiced? Because it may be that we're not performing not because the culture's the problem, but because we're not practicing it in the right way.

But it's not just the culture survey. At Gore, and at Menlo Innovations, and in every Thriving Organization, a variety of formal and informal practices are dedicated to making sure that the culture is continuing to work the way it's supposed to work.

So, yes, there are certainly advantages to starting from scratch, to being what we might call a "DNA Thriving Organization," but even these organizations must deal with the ongoing challenge of building and sustaining a *TO Culture*. And not surprisingly, the challenge is even greater for organizations where the existing culture is different from and even antithetical to a *TO Culture*.

So how do you tackle *that* challenge?

OPTION I:
THE BURNING PLATFORM

Changing an organizational culture is hard. For one thing, as we've seen, an organization's culture is based on several layers of not always visible, not always consciously held axioms, values, and principles. For another, it's just not easy for us as human beings to stop doing what we've been doing for a long time, especially when what we've been doing has been pretty successful. In fact, it's hard for us to change even when we haven't been especially successful, despite the common definition of insanity as doing the same thing over and over again and expecting a different result.

But these days, with all the interest in corporate culture, if and when an organization's leaders perceive that the organization is facing a very serious problem, they may well decide that culture change is at least part of the solution. They may also decide that the only way to make that

When we talk about organizational culture in this book, we're generally focused on culture at the enterprise level. But much of what is true at that level is also true for subgroups within a larger organization—for divisions, business units, departments, even for teams.

change happen—the only way to get everybody on board and overcome people's natural resistance to change—is to go into crisis mode.[9] Put a high-level team together to assess the problem, define a solution, lay out an action plan, set milestones, and assign responsibility. Make it clear to leaders at every level that this is a TOP PRIORITY. Create a sense of urgency—a "burning platform." And then just go out and do it.

That's what's going on in this cartoon.

"TIMKINS — I WANT A COHERENT NEW CORPORATE CULTURE THAT WILL TAKE US INTO THE THIRD MILLENNIUM AND I WANT IT BY THIS AFTERNOON."

In the cartoon, it's funny. In real life, not so much. Once they've gone into crisis mode, the organization's leaders may be sorely tempted to grab a solution off the shelf. Find a company that's known for having a great culture, figure out what they do, then copy it. "How about

---

9   In his 1995 book, *Leading Change*, John Kotter laid out his highly influential 8-step process for organizational change. Step 1: Create a sense of urgency.

Menlo Innovations? They're a software company, and we're a software company. They have a great culture. Let's go see them."

So the team goes off to Ann Arbor to spend time at Menlo, and they get excited about what they see. As soon as they get back, they convene an all-hands meeting to explain how the new culture will work. They redesign the workspace, put teams to work side by side around moveable tables, and post weekly project tasks and assignments on the walls for all to see. They even order the same corkboard that Menlo uses on their walls! Then they wait for the culture to change, and along with it, performance to improve. (Yes, I'm oversimplifying here, but from what Rich Sheridan has told me, probably not that much.) And by this point in the book, you know what's going to happen—not much, except maybe to cause some disruption, because they've focused on the top layer of the cultural iceberg, and not on what's under the surface.

By its nature, the burning platform approach is designed to generate a solution as quickly as possible. Not only does this encourage the organization to focus on practices and artifacts, but it makes it difficult to make a case for working on the deeper levels of the culture, because that work inevitably takes time. But the fact is, you can't just snap your fingers and have people suddenly change their (often unconscious) axioms and values-in-use.

Another problem with the burning platform approach is that it can easily lead to burn out. Once it becomes apparent that the way to get management's attention is to demonstrate that there's a crisis, lots of things get labeled that way. Want to get something done? Declare we have a burning platform. But then, before that crisis has really been dealt with, two or three other crises have been identified, each one requiring urgent action. Of course, there's only so long that people can operate at a fever pitch. Eventually—and certainly in the case of culture change, long before real change has occurred—change fatigue kicks in, and soon, people are just going through the motions. The fire burns out, and when that happens, the long-established axioms, values, and principles of the old culture rise from the ashes. (Sorry about pushing the "fire" metaphor so hard. I'll stop now.)

This is not to say that the burning platform approach is never appropriate. If an organization's environment has shifted so much that it needs to completely redefine its strategic intent and then morph the culture to serve that new strategic intent, then a sense of urgency may well be necessary. (One can only wonder if Kodak could have awakened in time to respond to the threat posed by digital cameras.)

And while real culture change always takes time to achieve and sustain, it's certainly possible that the intense initial effort generated by a burning platform approach will create at least some positive results in the short term. There may be an upward bump in the annual employee satisfaction survey and maybe an uptick in various performance metrics. Just the fact that the organization is paying attention to the problem can create a temporary improvement. If that happens, however, the tendency may well be to declare the culture changed and the problem solved. "It may not be perfect, but it's good enough. And there are other crises to deal with. Time to move on." And soon, once again, the old ways of doing business reestablish themselves.

So, while I appreciate that some dissatisfaction with the status quo may be involved in any successful change initiative, I don't generally recommend the burning platform approach. On the other hand, if an organization is truly facing a crisis, it's probably inevitable that its leaders will take that approach. If they do, they need to be keenly aware of the dangers of premature burnout, loss of momentum, and cultural backsliding. If they keep these in mind, if they resist the temptation to just fiddle with the top layer of the iceberg, if they put some real effort into understanding and shifting the underlying axioms and values, if they force themselves to stick with the program—regardless of whether it produces short-term results—then they might succeed in moving the organization at least somewhat closer to being a Thriving Organization. They might create enough change to give themselves and people across the organization a vision of how much more is possible. And that's no small thing.

But, that said, we should still take a hard look at another approach.

OPTION 2: PURSUING THE DREAM

Suppose an organization is *not* facing a crisis? Performance in some areas may not be what it could be, but there's no existential threat looming on the horizon. And yet, the leaders have a dream—a vision of something better. They want to create a Thriving Organization—one that will take its performance to a significantly higher level while—and *by*—enabling its people to more fully develop and apply their capabilities (for the organization's benefit as well as their own). What then?

In a situation like this, the leaders could still decide to pursue a burning platform approach. They could call everyone together and make clear their belief that building a Thriving Organization—which will require changing the existing culture—is VERY IMPORTANT, and urge everyone to get behind the effort.

If, after all, the organization is more or less successful, it may not be easy to sell everyone on the idea that significant change is needed. And even if the leaders do succeed in creating that sense of urgency, they will still face the problem of focusing too much or even exclusively on practices and artifacts.

But there is another option—a better option I believe, especially when there's no real crisis looming. This "pursuing the dream" approach is well illustrated by what has happened at CHG Healthcare.

As we've seen, CHG provides temporary staffing of doctors and other healthcare professionals. Most employees spend their days on the phone recruiting either new clients (in CHG's case, mostly hospitals) or appropriate medical specialists to meet those clients' needs. It's not easy work, and as a result, industry turnover is high. typically running between 50 percent and 60 percent.

In 2001, CHG's turnover was running at 49 percent (actually better than the industry average, which runs between 50 percent and 60 percent.) They were essentially losing and replacing half the workforce every year.

At that point, CHG's CEO began wondering what might happen if that rate were reduced. After all, the company's success depended on the relationships its employees developed with the clients and medical professionals they dealt with every day, and when those employees walked out the door, it was estimated that about 30 percent of those relationships went with them. Given that CHG's turnover rate was arguably less than most of their competitors, and given that the company's performance on a variety of key metrics was certainly acceptable, there was no crisis involved. But what if things could be better?

With that in mind, the CEO asked Kevin Ricklefs, then the HR director, to look into the issue. Kevin began by talking to managers in CHG's various offices, most of whom tended to respond with something like, "What's the problem? Our turnover is below industry levels." And if turnover *was* a problem, the implication was that Kevin, the HR guy, was the one who had the problem if he couldn't figure out a way to fill the empty seats faster.

Faced with this less-than-helpful input, Kevin figured he might learn something by talking to the employees themselves, so he set up a series of ad hoc focus groups. As it turned out, the employees had a great deal to say, not the least of which was that many of the managers just weren't very good at managing people.

It wasn't hard for Kevin to see that that perception of the company's managers was undoubtedly contributing to the high turnover. But he also knew that addressing that leadership issue would take time. Some deeply embedded axioms, values, and principles would have to change.

As it turned out, in the focus groups, Kevin had also gotten an earful about old chairs. As the company had grown, it had bought new chairs for the new employees, but it had never replaced the previous employees' chairs. In effect, about half of the staff were sitting pretty, while the others were not. And when you're on the phone all day, the chair you sit in makes a difference. So CHG's leadership grabbed the low-hanging fruit and replaced all the old chairs in one quick move— a simple fix that bought them time to work on the larger, underlying leadership issue.

Without doing anything more than asking employees for their input and responding to just one of their ideas, CHG moved the needle on turnover. In 2002, it dropped to 45 percent (again, from 49 percent the year before). Then, in 2003, the company began retraining its managers and launched a formal employee survey to continue the conversation begun in the focus groups. And lo and behold, turnover dropped again, to 39 percent in 2003.

Since then, CHG has remained committed to what Kevin Ricklefs describes as "an ongoing conversation with every employee that is two-way, open, honest, and focused on continuous improvement." As a result of that conversation, the culture has changed at every level, and turnover has continued to drop—to its current 15 percent. At the same time, the company has experienced consistent, significant growth. Today, CHG is the nation's largest provider of temporary medical staffing, and the second-largest overall provider of healthcare staffing services, with annual revenues in excess of $1.5 billion per year. It's also a perennial *Fortune* magazine Best Place to Work.

What can we learn from CHG's experience, and what can we conclude about the pursuing the dream approach to culture change. Well, for one thing, it takes time. During that time, the organization has a chance to look closely at its underlying axioms and values-in-use. It has time to help its leaders at every level develop a *TO* mindset. In CHG's case, over the years, the company has developed an award-winning leadership development program that helps leaders carry on that ongoing conversation with employees. [xxi]

The pursuing the dream approach also gives the organization's employees time to develop the deep trust that enables them to speak honestly and openly about the organization—and it gives the organization time to act on those ideas without disrupting day-to-day operations. It also gives the organization ample opportunity to learn as it goes—to try this, change that, on the basis of results over time.

You decide. Is pursuing the dream a better way to go?

NAVIGATING SUCCESSFUL CULTURE CHANGE

Every organization that's large enough to include various subunits is likely to have multiple cultures operating within its structure. The overall enterprise culture influences, constrains, but doesn't necessarily prevent the development of different cultures within some or all of the subgroups. Even a small team has its own culture, which will—perhaps more, perhaps less—mirror the enterprise culture.

Which means, of course, that leaders at every level have an opportunity to shape the culture of their particular unit. As Joe Patrnchak, the former Chief HR Officer at Cleveland Clinic, frequently says, "You are the CEO of your own organization, however large or small it happens to be."

We've just taken a high-level look at a couple of different approaches leaders can take if and when they decide that their organization's culture needs to change—if and when, hopefully, they decide that they want to transform their particular unit into a true Thriving Organization. In this chapter, we'll lay out a set of principles that will help those leaders in their efforts to make that transformation a reality.

Before we do that, however, let me say that these principles are built on, require, and help develop three very important personality characteristics of effective culture activists. The first is *self-confidence*. Not arrogance or an inflated sense of self, but a realistic assessment of what you can do. Without that well-grounded self-confidence, you might overreach and flame out, but what might be even more of a loss to you and the organization, you might well underreach and not even try.

The second characteristic of a successful change agent is what social psychologists refer to as *self-efficacy*. This is related to self-confidence, but it speaks to our belief that in certain kinds of situations, we know what to do or can figure out what to do so that we anticipate being successful. Self-efficacy is dependent on our sense of mastery, and our capacity to persevere—without which we certainly can't meet the challenge of sustaining successful change over time.

The third characteristic is *self-responsibility*. As we've already seen in our discussion of the values-in-use of Thriving Organizations, self-responsible people accept that they have weaknesses as well as strengths. They understand that they will make mistakes, that they won't always have sufficient wisdom to make the right decision, but they don't see themselves as helpless, as victims unable to make things happen. They initiate; they act; they do what they can do.

Self-responsible individuals tend not to get caught up in blaming others. Not that others don't have a responsibility as well—and the self-responsible person can help others see their responsibility by pointing it out to them—but self-responsible people look to their own motives, assumptions, and actions to see what part of a problem or a difficult situation they own.

So, recognizing the importance of these personal characteristics—self-confidence, self-efficacy, and self-responsibility—here are 12 principles that can help leaders build and sustain a *TO Culture*.

I. BE CLEAR ABOUT YOUR PURPOSE—AND ACT ACCORDINGLY

One way to approach life, metaphorically speaking, is to shoot at the wall and then paint a bull's-eye around the spot you hit. On the other hand, you could pick the spot you want to hit, paint a bull's-eye around it, take careful aim, and fire. And then, if you miss, adjust your aim and try again until you hit your mark.

Scott Beck, the CEO of CHG Healthcare, often gets asked by other leaders how to build a great culture, and if he would mentor them to help them do so in their own organization. In reply, he asks if they're serious, and when they inevitably say yes, he says, "Show me your calendar." If the calendar shows they're busy with product review meetings and sales meetings and meetings with the accountants—meetings all the way down, so to speak—with little or no time regularly scheduled for people stuff—coaching; helping develop the organization's leaders; talking to people across the organization about their work, about what's getting in the way of their succeeding, about their concerns, about how the organization is or isn't helping them grow and develop—then he'll question the person's seriousness. He'll question whether their purpose really is to build a great culture, because if that were the case, that should be reflected in their daily priorities.

So, you need to ask yourself if you really do want to take on the challenge of building a *TO Culture*. Why make the effort? And you should take this question of purpose down to a more personal level. What will you, personally, get out of building a Thriving Organization? What do you really want out of your work life? What do you want out of your life? How do the goals in your work life relate to your life goals?

If you're not clear about these things, you're just firing blindly at the wall.

In 2010, Clay Christensen gave the commencement address at Harvard Business School, later published in a book titled *How Will You Measure Your Life?*[xxii] He talked about a "vision of sorts" he had when he was a CEO. In his mind's eye, he had seen "Diana" a talented, hardworking, and valuable scientist/manager who was often frustrated because the company couldn't provide the equipment needed to satisfy all the demands others made on her team. He envisioned her leaving work after a hard, 10-hour day feeling discouraged and unappreciated, and he imagined the negative impact those feelings must have had on her family. And then he fast-forwarded to another scenario, in which the organization gave her the support she needed to succeed, enabling her to go home feeling "that she had learned a lot, having been recognized in a positive way for having achieved something valuable, and played a significant role in important initiatives." And he imagined how *those* feelings would affect her and her family.

At that moment, Christensen realized that, "If done well, management is one of the most noble of professions." He understood that leaders "have the opportunity to frame each person's work so that, at the end of every day, your employees will go home feeling like Diana felt on her good day." And at that moment, his purpose became clear.

As I've said more than once, culture change—building a *TO Culture*—is never easy. If as a leader you're not absolutely clear that that's what you want and need to do, if you're not absolutely clear about how that relates to what you do every day, if you're not absolutely clear about how it relates to your purpose, you might as well not bother even thinking about it.

2. IDENTIFY YOUR CIRCLE OF INFLUENCE

As we said above, self-efficacy is about having a realistic appreciation of what you can accomplish in any given situation. Stephen Covey talks about this in terms of a "Circle of Concern" and a "Circle of Influence." The former is made up of those many problems and issues that you would like to see dealt with, but which realistically you can do little or nothing about. Within that circle is your smaller "circle of influence," which includes those problems to which you could conceivably provide a solution. I may be greatly concerned about global climate change, for example, but practically speaking, I can probably only influence my family's, and perhaps my local community's, efforts to transition to re-newable energy sources.

Let's suppose you're the head of a department within a large, tradi-tionally bureaucratic enterprise. You may be very concerned about the overall enterprise culture, but realistically, all you can directly influence is your department's subculture. The question is how do you exert that influence? And, of course, the answer to that is by getting others to buy in, getting them to join you and help you in making your vision of a Thriving Organization into a reality.

That, in turn, raises the question of which members of the organization you can influence in that way. People who don't report to you, directly or indirectly—like your boss, for example, or people outside of your department—probably lie outside your circle of influence. That's not to say that you can't influence those people at all, depending on your relationship with them, your reputation and track record, your powers of persuasion, and so forth, but don't overestimate what's possible in that regard.

Obviously, the people most likely to be in your circle of influence are the people in your organization who report directly to you, although even some of those folks may have one foot in and one foot out of the circle. You know who I'm talking about—the folks who are experts in the art of passive resistance, the folks who say "Yes" when they really mean, "I'll just wait until this latest new thing dies a natural death."

And what about the other people in your organization, those who don't report directly to you? Suppose your department consists of 100 people, including 10 supervisors who are your direct reports. In that case, your circle of influence includes those 10 supervisors, although perhaps to varying degrees. But as for the other 90 people, their immediate supervisor will typically have more direct influence over them. By the way, this applies even to CEOs, who often think their circle of influence extends across the entire enterprise, when, in reality, it's much more limited than that. As far as significant direct influence, it's probably limited to the handful of senior leaders at the top of the organization who interact with the CEO more or less daily.

Of course, there is such a thing as indirect influence, and you should certainly do what you can to build more of it. To do that, you'll have to be *present*. You'll have to reach out and touch people. Bill Gore wandered the plant floor talking to people. Rich Sheridan at Menlo Innovations sits right in the middle of his organization, engaging all the time with its people. Scott Beck, CHG's CEO, gets out of his office regularly to take the pulse of the organization and give people a chance to talk directly to him. Don't expect people to trust and follow you just because of your title and formal authority. If you do, you'll end up sorely disappointed.

So, think carefully about your circle of influence. Think about the people who really should be in there, but who nonetheless seem unlikely to buy into what you're trying to do. What can you do to change that situation? If that ultimately proves impossible, and if their steadfast (albeit passive) resistance proves to be a real barrier to your moving the organization in the direction it needs to go, you may need to talk to those folks about moving on.

Generally, your time and energy will be better spent marshalling the folks who are already on board, or at least open to the idea, rather than trying to convert the unconvertible. Some of them may end up joining in when they see success. Some may choose to leave. But you can't let them exercise veto power over your initiatives through their resistance.

The most important thing here is not to overestimate or underestimate your circle of influence. If you're the CEO, and you think you can just demand "a new culture that will take us into the third millennium by this afternoon," you are vastly overestimating your circle of influence. By the same token, if you're only a team leader or department head, don't assume there is nothing you can do until those above you initiate action.

3. BECOME CULTURE SAVVY

I know it sounds obvious, but the more you know about organizational cultures, and the more familiar you are with the various models of organizational culture that have been developed, the more successful you're likely to be in building the culture that works best for your particular organization. By all means, start with the *TO Culture* model we've developed here, but just as my colleagues and I have drawn from many sources in creating it, you should also draw from other sources. A great deal of outstanding work related to organizational culture has been done over the years. Tap into it.

Read Schein's *Organizational Culture and Leadership*. That's a must. Dive into the Center for Innovative Cultures' booklist that we've included at the end of this book. Familiarize yourself with the work of people like Kim Cameron and Robert Quinn (at the University of Michigan's Center for Positive Organizations), and their "Competing Values Framework." Daniel Denison's highly regarded work on the "four key cultural traits of an effective organization" is well worth studying. By all means, get familiar with Gary Hamel's work: Gary has established the Management Innovation eXchange, where scholars, thought leaders, and business folks can interact on problems, ideas, and practices to improve the culture in organizations. And, please, be in touch with us at the Center for Innovative Cultures and find out about our programs.

Again, a great deal of excellent work has been done in this area, and the more you familiarize yourself with that work, the more effective your culture-building will be.

4. FIGURE OUT WHERE YOU ARE RIGHT NOW

So, let's say you've thought deeply about your purpose and have become committed to creating or helping to create a *TO Culture* in your organization. You've done your research and developed a pretty clear picture in your mind of what that culture will look like. You've thought about your circle of influence to identify the people you can count on to help you get there.

That's all great, but before you go ahead and launch on the culture change, you need to know where you're starting from. Ask yourself where your organization and its members fall on the Thrive-Thrive Matrix. (We've included some simple tools at the end of the book to help you with this.) Start with, but go beyond, the obvious performance metrics. Try to get a handle on how the organization fits into its competitive environment. What's happening, internally and externally that could affect the organization's future success? Examine the organization's engagement-disengagement profile. What percentage of people seem to be wilting, surviving, or thriving?

And, for sure, go out and talk to people—people in the organization and outside people who interact with it regularly—customers, suppliers, partners, and so on. Ask what they like and don't like about the organization and its culture—what strengths and weaknesses they perceive. Listen! Remember how CHG started its culture change by talking to, and listening to, its people? There's a lesson there.

One of your key goals is to understand where the organization's strategic intent, practices, processes, structures and deeper cultural elements may be misaligned. Remind yourself that what may have worked five years ago may no longer work as well; what was imported with great excitement from some industry leader may not work as well in a different context. You need to know whether your processes and structures are enabling or hindering the strategic intent of the organization. You need to know if they are aligned with or contradict *TO* principles, values-in-use, and axioms.

The point is that you shouldn't just rely on a gut feeling that your organization's culture needs to change. By itself, that's not enough—which brings us to the next step.

5. GET HARD DATA

If you need to persuade people, if you want to influence them, you need to tell a good story, but you also need to "speak with data." It's one thing to paint a picture of a glorious future, or to tell your organization's leadership team that the culture is toxic or not conducive to innovation. But your argument will be much more compelling if you can point out, for example, that only 15 percent of the organization's members are highly engaged—and then tie that piece of data to the organization's 25 percent attrition rate and its 40 percent decline over the past three years in new products brought to market.

As we saw at Gore and CHG, employee surveys can be extremely helpful in building a business case for change, deciding how to implement the needed change, and assessing the results. Surveys allow you to aggregate input from even a very large group of people. You can also use that aggregated data to benchmark your organization against some relevant reference group, although you need to do that very carefully.

But survey data is not the only kind of data you can gather. Focus groups provide qualitative data that is extremely useful in fleshing out survey data, and they can also help you beforehand in deciding which questions to ask in your surveys. The same is true of the less formal collection of qualitative data by just talking to people, one-on-one or in very small groups. For example, I've always liked getting the perspective of recently hired employees who haven't yet learned how to conform to all of the cultural norms that everyone else in the organization takes as second nature. You can learn a great deal by asking these "newbies" how your organization is similar to the last organization they worked in—and how it's different.

The nice thing about survey data, of course, is that it looks "hard." The quantitative data that surveys produce can be especially compelling in organizations that pride themselves on being numbers-driven. But you can approximate this with qualitative data, by taking care to capture what people tell you. Then you can analyze what you heard and make statements like "I talked to our 15 largest suppliers and 10 out of the 15 voiced some complaint with our accounts payable process. Specifically, they said . . ."

And, by the way, getting the data isn't important only as a way to get others to buy into the culture change you think is necessary. It's also crucial in helping you figure out your organization's specific cultural issues—where, for example, the espoused values and values-in-use may be misaligned. In many cases, it will help you pinpoint otherwise hidden stress points (like those uncomfortable chairs at CHG).

All of this is just another way of saying that the more you know, the more effective you can be.

6. NETWORK

Building a *TO Culture* is the work of many people. You can't do it alone. So you need to find and connect to people inside and outside of your organization who can help. You talk to one person, they suggest you talk to someone else, that person points you to someone else, and soon you have a working network of people with the skills and influence to help you succeed.

By all means, start close to home by networking within your organization. And here, I'm using "organization" in broad terms, to include your particular subunit as well as the larger enterprise. Look for like-minded and like-hearted people who want to create the same kind of Thriving Organization that you want to create. Look for people who see what needs to change, but who remain positive and optimistic that change is possible. Believe me, you're going to need those folks.

But don't stop there. As we've seen, there are many people out there researching organizational culture issues. And there are many people out there who are already involved in building and sustaining *TO Cultures* in their organizations—people like Rich Sheridan of Menlo Innovations and Scott Beck of CHG, and the leaders of companies like those in *Firms of Endearment*.

Don't just read about what these people are doing, although as we said above, that's a great place to start. My advice is that you find ways to connect with these people, talk to them, visit their organizations, add them to your internal network of people who can help you develop, refine, and execute your own ideas of how to turn your organization into a Thriving Organization. At the Center for Innovative Cultures, we sponsor a number of events every year that bring people together for this express purpose, and I can tell you that it's a very powerful learning experience for everyone involved.

I'm pretty sure that you'll find, as I have, that as busy as these people are (like you, they've got research to do or businesses to run), they're eager to talk about what they're doing because they care so deeply about it. In his book, *Joy, Inc.*, Rich Sheridan says that when he and his cofounders launched Menlo Innovations, they resolved to ". . . teach others about the joyful practices and systems we had conceived." You can and should take advantage of this kind of passion and intellectual generosity.

7. INDENTIFY THE "POSITIVE DEVIANTS" IN YOUR ORGANIZATION

Generally, we associate the word "deviance" with something negative. But the concept of positive deviance points to the fact that, in any organization, facing almost any problem, there's almost always at least one person who is already working in a positive way to address the issue. Find out who that person is in your organization and learn what they are doing!

Finding your positive deviants is like benchmarking, but instead of looking at the best practices in other organizations, you look for the best practices in your own. That's important, because as we've already discussed, when it comes to culture-related issues (and that covers an awful lot of territory), it's easy to pick up ideas that aren't culturally compatible, ideas that your organization will reject as soon as you try to implement them. On the other hand, if someone is making something work somewhere in your organization, there's a good chance that whatever they're doing could work in other parts of the organization.

That's not to say there isn't a place for benchmarking and learning from others: it's important to "cultivate a savvy sensitivity to the outside world." But it's just a reminder that what works somewhere else may not be as useful to you as something that's already working closer to home.

8. BUILD YOUR SKILLS

This is all about self-efficacy again. If you're going to lead successful culture change, you're going to need some serious skills. You'll need great sensemaking skills to figure out just what's going on in your own culture. You'll need great storytelling skills to paint a picture of what could be. You'll need great communication skills to convey in a clear and compelling manner how and why the organization needs to change. You'll need great persuasion skills to convince others that they should join you in making that change happen. People aren't born with leadership skills. You can learn the skills that you most need to build a Thriving Organization.

Let me tell you a brief story about David MacLeod, a British business leader, formerly a division CEO for ICI (Imperial Chemical Industries), the UK version of DuPont that was acquired by AkzoNobel in 2008. At about that time, David led an inquiry for the British government into why the UK had one of the lowest rates of workforce engagement among the 20 or so top industrialized countries in the world. The report, published in 2009, led to the formation of a UK initiative called Engage for Success, dedicated to helping British companies improve their employee engagement.

As part of this ambitious undertaking, David has had the chance to meet with many UK business leaders, and he tells this story:

> *When I talk to these people, it's not that they deny there's a problem. And it's not that they don't agree that we need to do something to increase the level of engagement. It's that they say, "David, I'm 60-something. I have maybe three to five years of runway left. In that time, I can do what I know how to do. I can acquire. I can*

merge. I can off-shore. I can squeeze out cost. What I can't do is change the Culture, *BECAUSE I DON'T KNOW HOW! And I don't have the time to learn and make it work."*

I understand where those leaders are coming from, although I'm not sure that they're not underestimating their self-efficacy. But I do know that this story makes me a little sad. If you don't want to find yourself someday regretting that you didn't build a truly Thriving Organization—if you don't want to find that you've missed the boat in achieving a purpose that went beyond accumulating a more impressive title and making more money—you need to build your skills. It's both necessary and possible to do.

9. GO FOR SMALL WINS

OK. You've done your research. You've collected the data and done lots of talking to—and more important, *listening* to—people inside and outside of your organization to get a good sense of what's going on in your existing culture, and what needs to change. You've sharpened your sense of purpose and your vision of what could be achieved. You've done some networking with people inside and outside your organization who can help you realize that vision.

Now you're ready to act!

But don't think that you have to do everything at once, or even that you have to tackle the biggest, most critical issues first. Don't forget CHG and those chairs.

The point here is to do something small now rather than take a long time planning something big. Think of what you're doing as experiments. During my time at Gore, one of the questions I heard most often was, "How hard would it be to try?" At Menlo, they say, "Let's run the experiment." As Rich Sheridan says: "The easiest way to describe this approach is to say, Let's try this and see what happens. If it works, do more of it. If it doesn't, change it or do less."

Of course, what's considered a small win will vary depending on the organization. When Cleveland Clinic began the work of changing its culture to improve employee engagement and the patient experience, one of the very first steps was to change the employee wellness program by making programs like Weight Watchers available for free and giving employees a $100 incentive just for participating in some kind of wellness activity. In an organization with 40,000+ employees, this initiative could be considered "small," but its cost would have been anything but small at a Menlo or CHG. The point is that by taking this first, small-in-this-context step, the Clinic immediately sent a message that it cared about its employees. The enthusiastic reaction—4,000 participants in the first six months, 13,000 in the first 18 months—helped build momentum for other steps, including the introduction of "servant leader" principles and the first enterprise-wide employee recognition program.

The data in Figure 8 also points to the power of small wins.[xxiii] It compares improvement suggestions made by Japanese and U.S. workers.

Figure 8. Comparison of Japanese and U.S. Employee Suggestions

Employee Suggestions	Japan	U.S.
Average net savings/adoption	$126	$6,114
Ideas/employee	37.4	0.12
Participation rate	77.6%	9%
Adoption rate	87.3%	32%
Net savings/100 employees	$422,100	$22,825

As the first line indicates, the suggestions of U.S. workers, on average, are potentially 50 times more valuable than those of the Japanese workers. But as you go down the table, you see that far more Japanese workers offer suggestions compared to U.S. workers, that the number of suggestions per employee is much higher for Japanese workers, and that Japanese companies adopt far more of the suggestions than U.S. companies do. The result is that the savings as a result of employee suggestions are much greater in Japanese companies. I find this table very compelling, not only for what it says about the "power of small," but also for what it suggests about the organizational cultural differences at work. For so many Japanese ideas to be adopted, there must be a lot of dots being connected that makes those ideas "good" ones.

10. INVITE OTHERS TO JOIN

OK, so small wins are important, but how do you make a big impact? One thing you do is persevere, and stay at it, à la CHG. But you also invite others to join in on the adventure. As Gary Hamel says, successful change is social. When Cleveland Clinic launched its Servant Leadership program, it found and trained a senior person in each major suborganization to be a champion for the concept. Over time, these champions encouraged people in their organizations to apply Servant Leader principles in resolving a variety of problems, and soon, Servant Leadership had gone viral.

You can think of this as a demand-pull approach, leveraging the results of successful experiments—the small wins—to build enthusiasm for culture change across the organization. Rich Sheridan talks about how this worked when he first tried out some of the ideas he later implemented at Menlo in another company. His team initially reacted with horror to practices like pairing up with one another and working in an open space. They begged him not to force them to do it. But then, two of his engineers volunteered to try the "paired development" idea and ended up embracing it. And that small something was the start of what turned out to be something very big.

So, leverage those small wins. Invite others to come along for the ride.

11. REFLECT ON WHAT YOU'VE LEARNED

All too often, when we've run an experiment or tried something—especially if it succeeded—we want to jump to the next idea on our To-Do list. Bad idea. Instead, after you've taken your first steps on the journey, take the time to think about what's been accomplished.

Think about what worked, what didn't, and why. Try not to get defensive about the things that didn't go so well. Try to open yourself up, to allow yourself to see and own the mistakes you may have made.

Think with one goal in mind: to learn what you can and figure out how to apply what you've learned to the next steps in the process. Because, remember, culture change *is* a process, and not always a smooth one. It will take time, and, in fact, it will never be completely finished. So, as Karl Weick famously says, "Don't just do something. Stand there!" At least until you know what to do next.

By the way, this is a perfect moment to invite others to join you, a perfect moment to engage your network, to get a broader perspective. And as you go through this process of reflection, remember, this is not an exercise in blaming others. It's not about making recommendations for others to follow. It's about asking yourself, "What am I going to do?" It follows from, and reinforces, self-responsibility.

12. REPEAT 1–11

Finally, it's time to do it all over again. Lasting change is not linear; it's cyclical. Hopefully, each cycle pulls in more people and has a greater impact. With each cycle, you learn more, add to your skill set, and increase your self-confidence and sense of self-efficacy.

Jim Collins calls this the "flywheel effect." You start small, see what works, experience the benefits, and do it again. In the process, you create a "virtuous cycle" that, over time, creates major, sustainable change.

A BRIEF SUMMARY

This seems like a good place to review the ground we've covered.

First, we discussed how and why it is that the traditional, bureaucratic organization, with its hierarchical, command-and-control structure, doesn't seem to work as well today as it once did. Today's organizations, at least in the industrialized world, must operate and compete in a very different environment. They must face such challenges as globalization; disruptive technological innovation; ever-accelerating change; and more highly educated workforces, made up of employees who are increasingly resistant to being treated as cogs in the machine.

We've seen that a new kind of organization is emerging, one that is committed to satisfying all of its stakeholders, not just its owners, and one where employees are given more opportunity to develop and make use of their unique talents, thus, making the organization more agile, more successful in coping with change. This is what we call the Thriving Organization.

Recognizing the critical connection between organizational culture and organizational performance, we've taken a close look at the Model of Thriving Organizational Culture. We've examined the core axioms, values-in-use, and principles that lie "below the surface" of this *TO Culture* while noting that they may shape practices and artifacts "above the surface" that vary considerably across organizations. And we've provided examples of how all this works in three Thriving Organizations in particular: W.L. Gore and Associates, CHG Healthcare, and Menlo Innovations.

In the last few chapters, we've taken on the issue of what it might take to change an organizational culture, to establish more of a Thriving Organization. That discussion included a couple of different approaches—a "fix it right now," burning platform approach and a pursue the dream approach based on a virtuous cycle of experimentation and small wins that build over an extended period into major, lasting change. Finally, we've laid out a set of steps that can help leaders at any level of an organization succeed in implementing successful culture change.

Now, let's move on to a ground-level look at our three selected Thriving Organizations. These mini-case studies are not intended to be comprehensive. You can learn more about Gore, CHG, and Menlo Innovations from the various books and articles they have stimulated. But what we've tried to do here is take you on a tour of each organization, pointing out the practices and artifacts that you might find unique and interesting. In some cases, we've made the connection to a particular axiom, value, or principle in the *TO Culture* model. In other cases, we've left it to you to do that for yourself.

So, let's start with Gore.

PART IV
MINI-CASE STUDIES:

W.L. Gore & Associates,
CHG Healthcare, and Menlo Innovations

W.L. GORE & ASSOCIATES

Note: While I continue to be in contact with and be informed by a number of Gore Associates, as I indicated earlier, the discussion of W.L. Gore in this book is drawn primarily from my direct personal experience over three decades with the company. Some practices at Gore have undoubtedly changed since I left in 2013. Jason Field, a 13-year Gore Associate from the Medical Division in Flagstaff, was recently advanced by the Board of Directors to be CEO, replacing Terri Kelly who retired at the end of March 2018. I am sure he will work to keep the culture appropriate for changing times. And with that in mind, I've chosen to rely heavily on the past tense in this case study.

Back in 1958 when Bill and Vieve Gore launched their business in the basement of their Newark, Delaware, home, the idea was to create something that was decidedly *un*-like the traditional bureaucratic organization. Remembering Bill's highly satisfactory experience as a member of DuPont's ad hoc, cross-functional task forces, what they had in mind was an organization that would stimulate and enable people to collaborate as effectively as possible. An organization where people—eventually called Associates—could get the information they needed when they needed it, without going through formal communication channels or a rigid chain of command. An organization where authority was not fixed, but fluid, depending on the task at hand.

And so, although it didn't receive its name until several years later, the Lattice Organization was born. And even as W.L. Gore grew from a few people in a suburban basement to a $3 billion enterprise with over 10,000 Associates in manufacturing plants and sales offices all over the world, that unique structure remained firmly in place. Over time, some fairly unusual practices were developed to ensure that the lattice structure would work the way it was intended—and as we've seen already in examples throughout this book, these practices grew out of the underlying axioms, values, and principles of Gore's *TO Culture*.

During my time at Gore, I often heard the company referred to as a leaderless organization, based on the fact that the company used almost none of the typical corporate titles—no directors, VPs, SVPs, EVPs, and so on. But if you asked Gore people about their culture, you were likely to hear, "We have leaders, but no bosses." This quip was based on Gore's idea of "natural leadership"—the idea that at Gore, people became leaders by attracting followers and sustaining that "followership" by their continued ability to help the group achieve its goals.

Most people outside of Gore, thinking in terms of a hierarchical model, tended to understand the notion of followers as equivalent to direct reports in a traditional organization. But at Gore, a networked organization, followers were not only the team itself, but Associates on teams that interfaced with that team and could even include the CEO, depending on the scope of the leader's responsibility.

The point is that Gore leaders—up to and including the CEO—typically didn't tell people what to do; they influenced and helped people do what all have agreed needs to be done. To get an idea of how this worked, let's look at Gore project teams, small units of typically 5–15 Associates. At Gore, teams were always at the heart of the organization (which reflects the *TO* axiom of making decisions at the lowest possible level). They were, to a very great extent, self-selected and self-managed.

Imagine that you were a Gore Associate, and you had an idea. It could be for a new product, a way to improve an existing business or manufacturing process, maybe even for a project like my original survey to find out how Gore Associates felt about the culture. You reached out to a few other Associates with relevant skills, experience, interests, etc. If people saw the value in the idea and committed to working on it with you, you most likely—although this wasn't guaranteed—became the leader of that team. That meant that those Associates not only thought your idea had merit, they also thought you had the capabilities to lead the team and the project to a successful outcome. But in keeping with the idea that at Gore, people can vote with their feet, if team members later lost confidence in your ability to take the project home, they could opt out, or suggest to you that it was time to pass the leadership on to someone else.

OK, so that's how natural leadership worked in small teams. But what about leaders with a broader scope of responsibility—plant leaders, business leaders, division leaders, and so on? The concept of natural leadership worked pretty much the same way for them too.

In the first place, most of these leadership roles were traditionally filled from within the company, and the only way to be selected for such a role was to have a strong followership, based on a proven ability to deliver results while doing things the Gore way. A great example of how followership influenced the selection of Gore leaders is what happened in 2005 when Terri Kelly took over as CEO from Chuck Carroll. Faced with Chuck's planned retirement, the Board asked the

Associates to submit the names of people they thought should take his place. From the input they received, it was clear that Terri had wide support throughout the Enterprise, and she was appointed. In her words, "It shocked the heck out of me."

There were certainly occasions when someone was brought in from outside the company because he or she possessed a background and skill set that seemed especially relevant to a particular challenge facing the organization. In these cases, though, the new person was usually given time and was always helped to build a core of followers before taking on that leadership role. Often, this meant spending months working within the organization they would—or more precisely, might—eventually lead, and only if and when they had developed a sufficient followership would they be asked to take on that role.

Leadership at Gore has always been more constrained than in a hierarchical organization. Gore leaders would typically avoid making any important decision, and certainly a significantly risky decision, without consulting with and gaining the support of other leaders and Associates. Again, leadership at Gore—certainly during my 30 years there—was less about figuring out what you wanted to be done and telling other people to do it. Rather, it was about working with people to figure out what needed to be done, and then helping them make it happen.

Over time, Gore developed a number of unusual practices. For example, in keeping with the ideas of enabling collaborative emergence and making decisions at the lowest level, plants and office sites at Gore were typically kept small. Generally, this meant 250 or fewer Associates, although that number might be as high as 400—still very small by the standards of most global enterprises. Even then, Gore tried as much as possible to create internal spaces that demarcate specific teams and businesses to keep the feel of a small plant.

A typical Gore plant was focused on developing, manufacturing, and selling products into a particular market space. When business grew to the point where the plant started to get too full (often signaled by the fact that it was harder to find a parking space in the plant parking lot and people were starting to park on the grass), Gore would break ground for another facility nearby. Although it would generally have been less expensive to expand the original facility, Gore perceived definite advantages in keeping each site small.

The tight focus at each site created an information-rich/information-relevant environment. By that, I mean that almost all of the information you needed to do your work was in the head of someone who worked at your site. You just needed to find that person, which was easy in a site small enough that people quickly got to know one another and learn each other's skills and temperaments. Trust was built, as was the sense of self-responsibility for plant performance.

Although "small is beautiful," there is also a need to take advantage of specialized equipment, knowledge, and know-how that might be hard to replicate in every single plant that needed it. So Gore adopted the practice of generally locating their small plants in "clusters," with anywhere from three to maybe 15 plants within a 30-minute drive of one another. In these clusters, you might have a facility devoted to fluoropolymer development, one where core IT infrastructure was housed, and another where legal or financial teams sat. Within any cluster, strong network ties connected Associates within teams, while weaker network ties connected teams within the same site to one another and to teams in other plants. It was a very effective way to ensure that information got to people who needed it as quickly as possible.

With so much information flowing through these networks, there was significant on-the-ground knowledge about various projects. As a result, when word got out that a new project was being championed by an

Associate with a good track record of accomplishment and great credibility, Associates were naturally drawn to it. (A pretty good example of "enabling collaborative emergence"?)

Gore's commitment to the common good and to treating each individual as a valuable contributor to the organization's success was manifested in many ways, including what the company referred to as "compensation for contribution." The idea was that in the interest of fairness, someone's compensation should be determined by the value they contribute to the Enterprise—and not by their level of education, seniority, the size of their team, and so on. (One of the things that had made Bill Gore chafe when he was at DuPont was that PhDs, by policy, made more money than those without that pedigree degree. Bill had an MS in chemical engineering.)

To make this system work, Gore employed a stacked ranking process in which Associates familiar with one another's work were asked on an annual basis to rank those colleagues, based on their contribution to the success of the Enterprise. It was left to the Associate to decide how to judge that contribution. For each group of Associates, an algorithm translated the Associates' combined input into a "contribution list," with the Associates at the top presumed to be making a greater contribution than the Associates at the bottom. Compensation decisions were made accordingly, with attention also paid to appropriate external benchmarks. The goal was to make compensation "internally fair and externally competitive."

But wait! Isn't that like the GE "rank and yank" process that has been mostly discredited? Didn't it lead to competition and in-fighting among Associates to make the top of the list? Actually, no.

For one thing, unlike the GE process, there was no presumption in the Gore process that those at the bottom of the contribution list were to be "yanked." There was no "The bottom 10 percent are gone." Second, and this is critical, the ranking was generated by the Associates, not just by the boss. How does that help? Well, if just the boss makes the compensation decision, then what I need to do is make sure I look good in the boss's eyes. That can certainly generate unhealthy competitiveness, and work against true collaboration and a sense of common purpose

But if my team is ranking me, and I'm the kind of person who looks out only for myself—for example, by stealing credit, badmouthing others, and withholding information or help that might be useful to another Associate—then regardless of what I may have accomplished my team is not likely to rank me very high in terms of overall contribution to the Enterprise. Indeed, the Associates who ranked high on most contribution lists were valued both for what they had accomplished personally, but also for how they helped others to contribute. They were *both* good individual players and good team players.

How did Gore people feel about this system? Well, I should say that in my discussions with hundreds, and quite possibly, thousands, of Gore Associates over the years, I mostly found that they preferred Gore's system to what they were used to or had heard about in other companies. They appreciated the fact that their compensation didn't depend just on the opinion of one person, i.e., the boss, using a performance evaluation process that often seemed arbitrary and even meaningless. They much preferred to have their contribution assessed by 10, 15, or 20 peers with whom they had worked on a variety of projects.

Of course, Gore went to great lengths to ensure that people with the *me-first* personality described above didn't get hired. When a team, plant, or other leader identified the need to fill a position, he or she would generally consult a few other Associates to see if they agreed, and then, acting as Hiring Champion, reach out to a member of the company's recruiting team. Together, they sketched out the job requirements, then invited three or four other Associates to fill out the hiring team. This group refined the job requirements, identified additional Associates to assist with interviews, and worked out who would ultimately own the hiring decision. Then the job was posted, internally and externally, and applicants brought in.

Gore's interview process was explicitly intended to provide a broader, richer understanding of each applicant's capabilities, experience, and interests. With this knowledge in hand, the hiring team might ultimately decide to go with one applicant over others because he or she seemed most likely to grow and add value to the company over the long term, even if it was not yet clear just what that might entail. In some cases, the team might reshape the current open position to take advantage of something a particular applicant brought to the table, or it might recommend an applicant for some other open position.

Like the compensation process, Gore's hiring practices took a fair amount of time, but they were specifically designed to ensure that the values on which the culture is based are preserved.

Many other Gore practices are well worth examining. For example, every Gore Associate, up to and including the CEO, had a "sponsor" from Day One.[10] Initially, the sponsor committed to helping the new Associate learn about the culture and meet other Associates who might be helpful to them. Over time, the sponsor provided feedback, served as a resource, and helped the Associate explore opportunities within the company that mapped to the Associate's sweet spot. This is the work or role that best aligns the Associate's interests and capabilities with the company's needs. Finding it is important in terms of giving each member of the organization the opportunity to thrive.

For many Associates, finding their sweet spot involved significant career shifts. As one Associate related:

---

10   Sponsorship is one of the Gore practices currently undergoing some modification. For example, Associates can no longer choose their own sponsor.

After college, I took an entry-level job at Gore in manufacturing. Through sponsorship, I was encouraged to try different things and spend time in other parts of the business, like accounting and scheduling, while being supported to grow and find my way with broad leadership responsibilities. Throughout my time at Gore, I found many sweet spots.

One last thought. Gore people have always been very aware of how the organization's culture affects their day-to-day experience. They are very likely to make their opinion known when they perceive that culture to be threatened by some proposed change in how the organization operates. And yet, the company needs to respond to changes in its environment. So, there has always been, and will always be, that tension between preserving the culture while unlearning the things that no longer work as well as they once did.

CHG HEALTHCARE SERVICES

Walk into any of CHG Healthcare's eight sites, and you'll see lots of people on the phone. CHG acts as a bridge between hospitals and clinics with a temporary need, and medical professionals willing to fill in temporarily, maybe because they like the idea of providing medical care in an underserved rural community, or because they just enjoy the lifestyle afforded by temporary assignments.[xxiv]

Roughly half of CHG's recruiters spend much of their time on the phone prospecting for clinics or hospitals (customers) in need of a temporary medical professional or collecting information from an existing customer about an opening. At the same time, the other half is on the phone looking for or discussing potential assignments with medical professionals who want to pursue temporary—so-called *locum tenens*—assignments.

But CHG's business also requires a great deal of collaboration. To make a placement work, recruiters from "both sides" of the organization must share information about the hospital's particular needs and the available medical professionals who might be appropriate for the assignment, the goal being to find the match that works best for both parties. And once the match has been arranged, a third CHG team is called upon to provide a whole host of services that make the placement possible—licensing, credentialing, malpractice insurance, housing, relocation, etc.—all requiring close consultation with the CHG recruiters involved.

When it all comes together perfectly, a kind of synergy occurs. Trust is built between the hospital and CHG, the medical professional and CHG, and among the CHG staff themselves. Those relationships generate repeat assignments and make the next assignment easier. They fuel the company's growth.

But making phone calls all day—with the inevitable non-response or rejection that entails—is a tough job. Recruiters have a daily quota of calls to make, most of which land in a voice mailbox. Even to get a call back can feel like a major accomplishment.

Not surprisingly, most businesses built around such work have a high turnover rate. As you may recall, more than 15 years ago, CHG's CEO decided to look into what, if anything, could be done about its 49 percent turnover rate (which no one saw as a problem, since the industry benchmark was even higher). That initial curiosity led to gradual but persistent changes in the CHG culture—changes that today make the company a perennial Fortune "Best Place to Work"—with a turnover rate of 15 percent, and some 18,000 applicants for 600 openings (in 2016).

If you ask CHG leaders about their culture, they will often point you toward its values. As the company website declares, "Putting People First is considered our defining core value and serves as our guiding light." The company's other espoused values are Integrity and Ethics, Quality and Professionalism, Continuous Improvement, and Growth. But it's clear from what goes on at CHG that its underlying axioms, values-in-use, and principles are very much those found in our *TO Culture* model.

Let's take a look at how those "below the surface" components of the culture manifest themselves in some of the company's practices and artifacts.

As we saw in a previous chapter, CHG's gradual transformation of its culture has been driven by their "ongoing conversation with every employee that is two-way, open, honest, and focused on continuous improvement." That conversation is facilitated by a number of practices.

There's the annual employee engagement survey, which contains both rating scales and space for comments. The 200+ pages of survey results are posted on the company intranet and studied carefully by CHG senior leadership, including Scott Beck, the CEO, who reads every comment. After taking the time to digest the results, the senior team produces a plan to address the issues. Scott then holds "town hall meetings" in all eight offices to discuss the survey results and the plan to address the feedback. Over the years, the survey has led to a variety of initiatives in direct response to what the employees have said they want and need from the company.

The engagement survey also includes questions designed to provide direct (although anonymous) feedback from the respondents to their own leaders. This input is passed on to the designated, individual leaders, who then go to the members of their organization for more feedback, and then develop a plan to address the issues raised. The first time an issue shows up for a given leader, it's considered "informational," and the leader is expected to figure out how to address it. Most of the time, they do. If the issue shows up again in the next survey, the leader is expected to meet with his/her own leader to develop a written improvement plan. In the rare cases where the issue continues to surface, the solution may finally be to move that person out of their leadership position and help them find something inside or even outside of CHG that is more suited to their skills and style. CHG takes employee feedback very seriously.

At CHG, however, an "ongoing conversation with every employee" goes far beyond an annual survey. There is, for example, a clear expectation that every leader at CHG will meet regularly with their direct reports, one on one. For most leaders, "regularly" ends up being every couple of weeks for half an hour to an hour; for others, it's once a week, and for others, it's once a month. But the key is that the employee always sets the agenda. If the employee wants to talk about her family or the vacation she just took, that's up to the employee. If the employee wants to use the time to talk about personal development possibilities, that's up to the employee. And if the employee wants to use the time to talk about issues he's having with the leader's style, that's up to the employee.

Now, even in organizations where leaders are expected to meet regularly with their employees, the template for that meeting is typically in the hands of the leader. As many companies (including CHG) have moved away from a yearly Performance Appraisal, the assumption is that leaders will use these regular meetings with employees to give feedback, raise concerns about performance, if warranted, and do some coaching.

CHG leaders are specifically trained in how to conduct "crucial conversations." But part of the reason CHG puts the agenda for much of the employee-leader conversation in the hands of the employee is that the company has somewhat upended the traditional leadership model, where the employee's job is to meet the leader's demands, and the leader's job is to hold the employee's feet to the fire.

CHG makes no bones about the fact that they are, in many respects, a traditional, hierarchical organization—unlike, for example, Gore and Menlo Innovations. But still, at CHG, as in those other Thriving

Organizations, the leader's job is to do what it takes to help their team members succeed. In fact, many of CHG's leaders speak explicitly about the company's Servant Leadership model. The team, including the leader, succeeds—or fails—together. No team success, no leader success. So it is incumbent on CHG leaders to listen to, and really hear, what their employees have to say.

Of course, employees, as much as leaders, have to buy into and commit themselves to this *team-first* mentality, and the role of open, honest employee-leader dialogue in making it a reality. That's why new hires at CHG come to the company's Salt Lake City headquarters for a week of onboard training that focuses on CHG's culture, values, and business model. The goal is to connect the dots—to ensure that every employee knows how CHG makes money, and how what they do and how they do it affects that outcome. In this very first week, each CHG employee also begins what will be continuing training in crucial work and life skills like building relationships, building trust, and how to have those "crucial conversations" in constructive ways.

Over the years, the ongoing feedback loop at CHG—that persistent effort of CHG leaders to learn from the employees—has led to the development of many of the company's practices and artifacts. As we've already seen, it has certainly led to a change in how leaders think and behave. But it can also be seen elsewhere.

It has led, for example, to a deep commitment to training and helping every CHG employee to thrive by developing their full potential. That commitment is made real by providing an average of more than 100 hours of training to each employee each year.

And then there's the work space. At Gore, small plants are one way the company facilitates collaboration and the unimpeded flow of information. At Menlo, the same goal is achieved via everyone's working close to one another at shared tables in one large, completely open space. At CHG, cubicles provide some privacy for all those phone calls—but unlike most call centers, CHG's cubicles are only three feet high, essentially the height of a desk.

CHG teams sit close by each other, and team members often call out to one another over their cubicle walls or roll their chairs from one cubicle to another when they need help or want to share a piece of information. No e-mail required. Sometimes the team leader will call a quick huddle, and everyone will stand for a brief exchange—often the announcement of some accomplishment. On occasion, people will sing or dance or move around to "de-stress"—all in good fun. (This last behavior might sound quirky, but quirky is normal at CHG. The dress code is always casual, and on any given day, some employees are likely to appear in some sort of costume. Again, it's all in fun.)

Having fun is definitely important at CHG, and along with that goes a willingness to celebrate. Charlie had a very successful week on calls. Celebrate! Maria has been with CHG for five years. Celebrate! Carmen completed a course or helped establish a new Employee Networking Group. Celebrate!

Every CHG leader has a celebration budget—which they're expected to use. That results in frequent planned and impromptu events—birthday parties, pizza parties, bowling outings, etc.—that help build team relationships. In addition to these small-scale events, CHG's Corporate Events team produces 400+ events every year. This includes the annual Employee Appreciation Week, with its Battle of the Bands, costume contests, and a whole host of other activities.

And then there is the President's Club, where folks who've met or exceeded stretch sales goals go off with their spouses/partners to a prime location for several days of recognition and celebration. What's interesting about the President's Club at CHG, unlike similar events at other companies, is that there aren't a finite number of "winners."

Anyone who meets or exceeds their stretch goals gets to go. This tends to discourage unhealthy competition and encourage cooperation and mutual assistance. If we help each other succeed, we'll all get to go!

As much as CHG's culture supports having fun, it also encourages something more like the "joy" that Rich Sheridan talks about at Menlo. And so, if you talk to CHG employees, they will often refer to the work they do as "making a difference." It's common to hear CHG people say, "What I do saves lives." This sense of a higher purpose is constantly reinforced by the telling of stories about the medical professionals CHG has placed, and how they have touched the lives of many people—more than 25 million patients every year.

CHG employees also "make a difference" through volunteer work in their local communities—work that the company supports by giving each employee 8 hours of paid time off to help out at the charity of their choice. It's called Volunteer Time Off, or VTO, and CHG employees donated 6,656 such hours in 2016. CHG employees also nominate teammates who regularly volunteer in their communities for the annual Making a Difference award, which sends a group of winners off to a place like Kenya to build housing, schools, or water purification systems.

Together, CHG's array of practices translate its underlying *TO Culture* into an environment that could otherwise be a stressful, repetitive "survive-wilt" experience into something far more positive. And the results have clearly paid off in terms of achieving the company's strategic intent, pushing it past its competitors, and producing an exceptional level of financial performance.

MENLO INNOVATIONS

In 2001, Rich Sheridan and James Goebel co-founded Menlo Innovations, a (now) 40+ person developer of custom software. Their purpose was nothing less than to "end human suffering in the world as it relates to technology."

Software developers spend long hours under great stress building applications to specs typically defined by marketing people whose understanding of what the customers want—let alone, need—is severely limited. The resulting product is often late getting out the door, and more often than not, so bug-ridden and hard to use that it leaves the end users tearing at their hair in frustration.

Pretty much every organization today uses software to run some or most aspects of its operations. Sometimes that software can be purchased "off the shelf" and configured for use: think Salesforce or SAP. In other cases, a standard package, however carefully configured, just won't meet the organization's needs. That's where Menlo Innovations comes in.

For example, a large, multibillion dollar healthcare system turned to Menlo after concluding that standard electronic medical records software simply could not manage all the patient-related information related to organ transplant procedures. Menlo's High-tech Anthropology® team worked with the healthcare system to design the user experiences needed by the doctors and nurses. Menlo engineers then built the software necessary to handle all the diagnostic, monitoring, and posttransplant information (while also interacting seamlessly with the organization's other information systems). The project took three and a half years, but a dozen years later, that software is still in use.

Rich is well suited to the task of making at least some of this pain go away. He grew up a computer geek in the '70s; he went to a high school that offered computer programming, and quickly became the go-to computer guy for his fellow students, as well as the school's teachers and administrators. After earning a degree in computer science from the University of Michigan, his career took off, his enthusiasm and smarts leading to bigger and bigger projects, more impressive titles, more money, and stock options. But by his own admission, by the late '90s, the joy was gone.

So, he tried an experiment. At the company where he served as the head of R&D, he set up a skunkworks in an open space that looked more like a factory floor than a typical software development lab with its warren of cubicles. He teamed up with James Goebel, then a consultant, to try different ways of having his developers collaborate, both with one another and with customers. At first, their ideas met with almost total resistance, but soon they seemed to take hold. As one of his developers said, "I am having so much fun, it doesn't feel like work anymore. I'm not sure you should pay me." For Rich, the joy was back.

But then the dot.com crash sucked the wind out of the IT industry, and Rich's parent company shut down his development shop. Unfazed, he and James decided that this was a great time to push their ideas even further—by launching their own custom-software company! Enter Menlo Innovations.

When you visit Menlo for the first time, it's a little disconcerting. You find yourself in a large open space in the basement of a multi-story parking structure in the center of Ann Arbor. No windows. No offices. No cubicles. A polished concrete floor. You might well find yourself wondering just exactly how this workspace contributes to Menlo's goal of enabling "joy" at work.

And then there's the noise! Everyone is working at five-foot aluminum tables, pushed together into "pods," people talking to the people around them, all contributing to the noise level. Every once in a while, someone shouts across the space: "Hey, Bill!" When Bill responds—without moving—a question gets tossed across the room, Bill answers, and no one else seems to notice. Occasionally, Rich Sheridan or someone else will call out, "Hey, Menlo!" Everyone responds with "Hey, Rich!" and suddenly you're in an all-hands meeting. Rich makes his announcement, a few people comment, and it's back to work. Like so much else at Menlo, this unique communication practice has a not-entirely-serious label: they call it High Speed Voice Technology.

And what's all this stuff on the walls? If you take a closer look, among all the pictures and posters, you'll find charts detailing the company's financial performance and projections. And then there are the "Work Authorization Boards," one for every project the company is working on. Each of these displays consists of 5x8 cards detailing the work for that week, one card for each day's tasks, by each pair of developers, all laid out for everyone to see. Hmmm. The whole idea of this place seems to be to have everybody know and be involved in everything.

If you happen to be at Menlo on the right day, you can see them re-configure the whole space, moving the tables around into new pods to optimize the current project work. (Cords and cables hanging down from the ceiling make this an easy process.) Each pod is dedicated to a specific project, and at each table in the pod, two developers work side by side, sharing one computer and one keyboard. This is the pairing practice so critical to how Menlo operates. The developers in each pair are constantly "speaking their thinking"—collaborating in real time, all the time. "How about if we try this?" "I don't think that's the way to go. Here's why." "Was there anything from last week's work that we need to watch out for as we write this code?"

As the pairs talk to each other, the other developers paired off in the pod can overhear them. When they hear something relevant to what they've done or what they're about to do, they may chime in with a question or a suggestion.

The pods are also situated so that Menlonians who might not be work-ing on a particular project, but who might have some insights to offer, are close by. That makes it easy for them to be called upon—and also for them to overhear something at a nearby pod that encourages them to jump in with some helpful input. The whole environment is context-rich, information-rich, and highly effective at keeping people informed about what's going on. It's a great way for people to learn from one another.

Cross-learning is also facilitated by Menlo's practice of shuffling the developer pairs every week! That way, relationships are constantly deepened and refreshed, knowledge about specific projects and new programming techniques is disseminated rapidly throughout the company, and the sense of community and shared purpose is enhanced.

As you might surmise, Menlo isn't big on meetings. There are three glass-walled conference rooms for use when it's necessary to talk to outside folks in a quieter space. Other than that, meetings tend to be of the "Hey, Menlo" variety. They do have a "daily stand-up," however. Every morning an alarm goes off, and everyone gathers in a circle. One developer pair starts things off by quickly telling the group what they're doing and what help they could use. While they're speaking, they hold a plastic Viking helmet between them by its horns. By itself, that's probably enough to keep them from going on too long. They pass the helmet to another pair, and the process repeats itself until the circle is complete. Typically, these "meetings" last under 15 minutes—but they serve the purpose, again, of connecting the dots and facilitating the flow of information and knowledge across the organization. (Beats e-mail, doesn't it?)

Menlo's commitment to "enabling collaborative emergence" is also manifest in their practice of integrating "High-Tech Anthropologists®" into everyday operations. Every project is assigned a pair (of course) of Menlonians who scour the customer environment for a clear understanding of the end user's needs. This isn't just pulling some end users into a focus group. It goes beyond that, because experience has taught Rich Sheridan and his colleagues that, at least when it comes to software, people often don't know what they want, don't know how they'll use something they think they might want, and have little appreciation for the value of some feature if they can't link it to what they want to do. The High-Tech Anthropologists spend real time in the real places where end users do their real work. They watch, they listen, they interact, and they develop a deep and nuanced appreciation for the way a new tool or piece of software might find a home (or not) in that particular work environment. And, of course, they bring that information back to the Menlo developers. Talk about cultivating a savvy sophistication of the outside world!

At Menlo, they give far more than lip service to the idea of keeping customers involved. For example, they invite customers in to work with the software as it is being developed. With the customer sitting at the computer, it quickly becomes apparent what works well and what doesn't. Presumably, the Menlonians are pleased when what they've done merits a "well done" from the customer, but they also seem genuinely pleased to find out where they need to do better. While they might not talk about it in these terms, this commitment to customer intimacy certainly reflects the company's belief in the core axiom of promoting the common good.

As you might imagine, Menlonians are very sensitive to the unique qualities of their culture, so they want to make very sure that the people they hire will fit into that culture. You can see that in their hiring practices.

Given the high value Menlo places on collaboration, their hiring process has to be about much more than technical talent. So the first "screen" for potential new Menlo employees, the kindergarten test, is: Do they know how to share? Do they play well with others? If the answer is no, then the candidate's skill level doesn't matter.

With this in mind, Menlo starts the hiring process with what it dubs an "extreme interviewing event." They bring in a whole group of potential new hires—perhaps as many as 30—on the same day. They give them an overview of Menlo—the company's values, how the work gets done, etc. They tell them that this first interview will determine who gets asked back for the second interview. Then they put them in pairs to work together on solving some paper and pencil problem.

Three times during the process the candidate pairs are shuffled. And here's the interesting part. They tell each person that as they are working on those assignments, their task is to make sure their partners get invited back for a second interview! Huh? You mean I'm not supposed to show off my programming chops!

Think about it. If everyone at Menlo is working to help others contribute as much as they possibly can, the total productivity of the team will be much higher. So, as the candidate pairs work, Menlonians watch. One observer is assigned to each group, so each candidate gets observed by three Menlonians. They see the person who grabs the pencil out of his partner's hand and starts working out the problem himself on a yellow pad. They see the person who asks for the pencil, sketches out an idea, and then asks her partner what he thinks of the idea.

At the end of the day, the Menlonians gather for a quick thumbs-up-thumbs-down exercise. If all three observers for a particular candidate give him or her a thumbs-up, that candidate is invited back. A unanimous thumbs-down and that candidate will be thanked for thinking of Menlo. Where there's a split, the whole team talks it through until a decision is reached.

The candidates who pass this first screen come back in for a day, during which they are paid to work with a Menlonian developer pair on an actual project. At the end of the day, if the feedback on the candidate is positive, they'll be invited back for a three-week paid internship, working just as if they were already on board. Only if that trial goes well will the person finally be offered a position.

Obviously, this all takes time. But let's not forget that a Thriving Organization is committed to investing in future capacity.

There's much more we could say about Menlo's culture, but instead, let me refer you again to Rich Sheridan's book, *Joy, Inc.* And as I pointed out earlier, every year, thousands of visitors head to Ann Arbor to see

Menlo's culture up close. That would be a great way to enhance your network building process.

But before we move on, let me leave you with one last story about Menlo. When one of its employees had a baby, she ran into a problem. She wanted to come back to work, since an exciting new project was starting, but the day care center she planned to use was full and not accepting new children at the time, and the baby's grandparents lived too far away to help. Rich suggested she bring the baby to work, a solution that no one, including the mom was sure would work. But as is so often is at Menlo, the decision was, "Let's run the experiment!"

And the experiment worked. At the time of my last visit, 18 "Menlo babies" had come into work with their moms and dads until they were old enough for day care. One of the few closed-off rooms off the factory floor has been turned into a sleep-and-nursing room for infants and moms. The little ones mostly sleep. But when they need someone to hold them and walk them around, there are dozens of "aunts and uncles" who are happy to pitch in. It's about collaborative emergence, right?

It's hard to feel that you're just a cog in the wheel when you are supported that way by your colleagues. And it's hard not to feel committed to the common good when you're walking the floor with someone else's baby.

FIRMS OF ENDEARMENT

US Public Companies
- 3m
- Adobe Systems
- Amazon
- Autodesk
- Boston Beer Company
- CarMax
- Chipotle
- Cognizant
- Colgate-Palmolive
- Costco
- FedEx
- Google
- Harley-Davidson
- IBM
- J.M.Smucker
- Marriott International
- MasterCard
- Nordstrom
- Panera
- Qualcomm
- Schlumberger
- Southwest Airlines
- Starbucks
- T. Rowe Price
- UPS
- Disney
- Whole Foods

US Private Companies
- Barry-Wehmiller
- Bon Appetit Management Co.
- Clif Bar
- Driscoll's
- GSD&M Idea City
- Honest Tea
- IDEO
- Interstate Batteries
- Jordan's Furniture
- L.L. Bean
- Method
- Millennium Oncology
- New Balance
- Patagonia
- Prana
- REI
- SAS Institute
- SC Johnson
- Stonyfield Yogurt
- TD Industries
- The Container Store
- The Motley Fool
- Timberland
- TOMS
- Trader Joe's

Non-US Companies
- BMW (Germany)
- Cipla (India)
- fabIndia (India)
- FEMSA (Mexico)
- Gemalto (France)
- Honda (Japan)
- IKEA (Sweden)
- Inditex (Spain)
- Mahindra & Mahindra (India)
- Marico (India)
- Novo Nordisk (Denmark)
- POSCO (South Korea)
- TCS (India)

APPENDIX 2.

MORE ABOUT ORGANIZATIONAL CULTURE

The *TO Culture* model discussed in this book draws heavily on Edgar Schein's groundbreaking work on organizational culture, as well as the work of many others who have explored this topic. I've personally been greatly influenced by Karl Weick's work on "sensemaking"—the ways that people in organizations make sense out of the events and experiences and data and stories that comprise daily organizational life. Weick emphasizes that we "make" meaning, we "make" sense, and in proactively doing so with respect to our organizational life, the organizational culture is itself one of the most important resources we bring to bear. Weick particularly elucidates how cultures evolve—often through seemingly small variations in sensing, interpreting, and creating responses to variations in the outside environment.

Two other scholars whose insights have been particularly influential in our development of the *TO Culture* model are Sonja Sackmann, currently on the faculty of the Universität der Bundeswehr München, and Deborah Ancona, Seley Distinguished Professor of Management in the Sloan School at MIT. Both have been active in developing models of organizations that contrast the traditional bureaucratic, hierarchical model with newer models where shared understanding, shared values, and shared leadership are more the mode of operating.

Now let's talk a bit more about how Schein's work has influenced the development of our *TO Culture* model, as well as some of the ways in which our model differs from his. Let's start with his definition of organizational culture as:

> *... a pattern of shared basic assumptions that was learned by a group as it solved its problems of external adaptation and internal integration, that has worked well enough to be considered valid, and therefore, to be taught to new members as the correct way to perceive, think, and feel in relation to those problems.*

What I find compelling about Schein's definition is that it points to an organization's culture as something dynamic, a product of what the organization has gleaned over time from dealing with significant challenges and opportunities. As those challenges and opportunities change, whether because of external or internal forces, the organization's continued success and even its survival depend on its ability to make appropriate changes to its culture. Thus, one of the biggest issues for organizations with strong cultures is their ability to *unlearn* what once was learned.

The next point I want to make is that while our model is obviously influenced by Schein's Iceberg Model, there are a couple of significant differences that need to be highlighted right up front.

First, there's the fact that Schein offered his model as a descriptive metaphor for any organizational culture. He wasn't saying anything about whether a particular culture, a particular set of practices or values or assumptions, are "good" or "bad," "right" or "wrong," "useful" or "not useful." He was just saying, this model represents the architecture of any organizational culture, with its multiple layers, some "above the surface" and easily visible, and others hidden below the surface.

Our model, on the other hand, is intentionally prescriptive. In offering it, we're arguing that certain specific values, principles, and axioms can, in fact, be considered "good," insofar as they are critical to the development of a culture that enables and sustains a Thriving Organization. As we've seen, the question of practices and artifacts is a bit more complicated, since they can, and should, vary so much from one Thriving Organization to another.

Another important way that our model differs from Schein's is that ours refers to values-in-use, as opposed to Schein's "espoused values." I'm not sure why Schein chose to focus on espoused values. Looking closely at organizations like Digital Equipment Corporation and Hewlett Packard, he rightly concluded that, "Beliefs and values at this conscious level will predict much of the behavior that can be observed at the artifacts level." But he also recognized that in many organizations, there is a significant disconnect between the espoused values and the values that people actually demonstrate in making decisions and taking action: "Thus a company may say that it values people and that it has high quality standards for its products, but its record in that regard may contradict what it says."

Just to be clear: in my view, if you really want to understand an organization's culture—and certainly, if you want to shape or reshape an organization's culture—you need to focus on the values that are actually in use across the organization, whether or not they are the espoused values. If there's a significant disconnect between the values-in-use and the espoused values, the likely result is a culture rife with cynicism and a high number of actively disengaged employees. You simply can't build a Thriving Organization with that kind of values disconnect.

Compared to Schein, we've also added a layer of "principles," the mental constructs that most directly operationalize the culture's axioms and values-in-use. The principles are the means by which what lies "below the surface" of the culture becomes manifest in its specific practices and artifacts.

In our model, we've also chosen to use the term "axioms" rather than Schein's term, "assumptions," for the ideas that form the bedrock of an organization's culture—the ideas that ultimately shape the organization's values, operating principles, practices, and artifacts. My sense is that "assumptions" often connotes relativism: these are your assumptions; these are mine. An axiom, on the other hand, is "true," or in an organizational context, it is at least accepted as true. In that sense, the axioms we've identified are necessary to the culture of a Thriving Organization.

APPENDIX 3.

CULTURE CHANGE TOOLS

THRIVING CULTURE SURVEY

On the following pages are a set of items you can use to see how close (or far) your organization is from the ideal high-performing organizational culture described in this book. Of course, no culture is perfect, and no organization will score high on every item. But this tool will allow you to get a snapshot of where you are right now, and where you might want to put energy into improving. (Note: A more sophisticated version of this survey is available online at www.innovativecultures. org.)

The items are arranged in three sections: assessing cultural principles, assessing cultural values-in-use, and assessing cultural axioms. In each section, for each item, there is a pair of statements that might be roughly opposites. Read both statements and then think about your organization. When you think of what you hear people say, is it more often like what's on the left side statement, or more like what's on the right-hand statement? When you think about your own reflections regarding what you say or think, is it more to the left or right?

	-3	-2	-1	0	+1	+2	+3	
1. I don't have a clue about what our mission is, or how what I do fits in.								1. I understand the mission of our organization and how my work contributes to it.

If one of the statements is absolutely dead-on in describing your organization, put a check in the -3 or +3 column closest to the statement. If both statements are about equal, then put a check in the 0 column. And if there's a tendency or a slight tendency toward one or the other statements, use the -2 or -1 or +1 or +2 columns.

When you complete the assessment, look to see where your checkmarks fall. The more to the left, the more work you have. The more to the right, the better shape you're in. Also, check whether your assessment reveals greater challenges as you go "down the iceberg." Lots of checks in the left-hand columns under axioms will suggest you'll have lots of major work to do. But if the axiom level and the values-in-use level are more in the right-hand column, you'll probably be able to make changes in principles with greater ease if you link the change to the underlying values or axioms.

You might want to get others on your team to fill out this survey as well, create an overall score for each item, and have people compare their scores with the aggregate score. What are the differences in experience that lead to different judgments?

A. Assessing Cultural Principles

	-3	-2	-1	0	+1	+2	+3	
1. I don't have a clue what our mission is, or how what I do fits in.								1. I understand the mission of our organization and how my work contributes to it.
2. I have no idea how we actually make money, and I'm not clear on how what I do helps.								2. I understand our business model of how we make money, and I can make decisions on what I do and how I do it aligned with our business model.
3. Leaders don't give us much of a big picture view of our business. Mostly I know just my team or unit, if that.								3. Leaders frequently provide a big picture overview of our business, how we're doing, and what our plans are.
4. The people making the big decisions here have no idea of what's happening on the front lines with customers, suppliers, or competitors.								4. The people making the big decisions here are well informed about what's happening on the ground and integrate that information into strategy adjustments as appropriate.
5. We get blind-sided a lot by our customers, suppliers, competitors, and regulators.								5. People outside of our organization often call upon us to provide a broader perspective on what's happening across our industry.
6. Even for smaller projects, most of the direction and even the way to go about doing it is set from above.								6. Teams have lots of opportunities to explore and try new ways of doing things or even try new things to do.
7. Collaboration isn't one of our strengths.								7. Collaboration is part of everything we do.
8. Around here, we don't like surprises—even good ones.								8. We're often willing to strike off in a direction even though we're not sure what we might find.

9. Efficiency is the name of the game here.								9. Innovation and being able to adapt to change is the name of the game here.
10. We pretty much work in isolation here, and there's not much encouragement to build relationships with others in the organization.								10. We are constantly encouraged to build stronger relationships among members of our team, and even among other members of the organization who aren't on our team.
11. If I have a suggestion for a new way of doing something, I might as well keep it to myself.								11. It's easy to experiment and try new things here.
12. Leaders pretty much operate in a command-and-control style here.								12. Leaders help us get things done.
13. I feel pretty constrained in what I can do or not do.								13. I feel like I have a lot of latitude to decide what to do and how to do it.
14. I'd be disinclined to challenge a senior leader on anything.								14. I feel free to speak my mind constructively regardless of who's in the room.

B. Assessing Cultural Values-in-Use

	-3	-2	-1	0	+1	+2	+3	
1. You can't trust what people say here.								1. Here, people keep commitments and do what they say.
2. I see a lot of people cutting corners and not being exactly ethical in this organization.								2. People here are honest and ethical and operate with integrity.
3. You have to watch out for yourself here. No one else will.								3. People care for one another here, especially when people hit difficulties or a hard time.
4. Here, people play favorites.								4. In this organization, people try to figure out what's fair to each person, to the team, and to the organization as a whole.
5. We're good at buck-passing and playing the blame game.								5. People here admit when they've made mistakes.
6. People here need to be held accountable.								6. People here hold themselves accountable.
7. There is a lot of "bitching and moaning" here.								7. We feel it is important to raise issues here and then to be willing to deal with them.
8. You don't get a lot of feedback here from anybody—your leader or your teammates.								8. People are pretty constructive in their criticisms here and offer it to help others get better.
9. Most people in this organization are focused on what they accomplish and let everyone else know.								9. There's a real appreciation here for the unique skills and talents that each person brings to help us all accomplish more.
10. People steal credit for anything good where they can claim they had a hand in it.								10. People thank one another for the contributions they make to our collective success.

C. Assessing Cultural Axioms

	-3	-2	-1	0	+1	+2	+3	
1. Many people here are treated disrespectfully.								1. I am treated with respect in this organization.
2. People in this organization are seen as easily replaceable and just cogs in a big machine.								2. People here are valued as unique individuals who all have the potential to grow and develop.
3. It's cutthroat here. Most decisions are very political.								3. I'd say we all understand and promote the "common good."
4. No one here wants to get to the end of the fiscal year with money left in the budget. If you have it, you spend it.								4. People are willing to have their resources shifted to other opportunities if there's a good explanation of why those opportunities are better for the whole.
5. Important decisions, and even some unimportant ones, tend to get pushed up the ladder.								5. If I have a good understanding of the situation and a solid reason for doing something, I can make my own decision.
6. We're in it for the quarterly numbers.								6. We're in it for the long term.
7. It's a job.								7. I'm proud of what we do here.

Assessing Your Practices

Think about the major practices (and artifacts) that visibly manifest your culture. They may be things like how you make hiring decisions, how you compensate people, how meetings are held, the size and location of offices, and who sits where in the cafeteria. They can be practices you are proud of, or that leadership is proud of, or that no one is proud of. But try to think of things that likely have an impact (positively or negatively) on how the culture is experienced. (You might reflect on practices that have a strong impact on the previous survey items.)

List them below, and then consider how the practice helps the strategic intent of the organization and the functioning of the culture, and how the practice hinders the strategic intent of the organization and the functioning of the culture. Note: Sometimes, a practice or artifact may both help and hinder, but in different ways.

As with the last tool, you might want to invite others to fill out their own version of the Practices Assessment and compare and discuss.

Key Practice	Ways It Helps	Way It Hinders

Assessing Organizational Health

The next step is to assess your organization's health by plotting it on the Thrive-Thrive Matrix. Remember that the two dimensions of the Thrive-Thrive Matrix are the organizational dimension—how well the organization is doing, and the individual dimension—how well individuals in the organization are doing. Also remember, the three main categories on each dimension are wilt, survive, and thrive.

First, determine the extent to which you think your organization is wilting, surviving, or thriving. You may make your holistic judgment based on metrics like: profit, sales revenues, profit growth, revenue growth, return on net assets, market reputation, market position, competitive differentiation, leadership reputation, and others.

Where do you see your organization?

Then, determine the extent to which you think the individuals in your organization are wilting, surviving, or thriving. Again, you may make your holistic judgment based on metrics like annual survey scores, recognition as a Great Place to Work, turnover, capacity to attract talent, and others.

Where do you see the individuals in your organization?

Given the size and complexity of your organization and your familiarity with the organization as a whole, you might not be able to give an overall score for the entire organization. You may know your division, but not the entire company. Or maybe even only your work team and not the entire company. You can make multiple assessments, each with greater or lesser uncertainty.

Next, plot your assessment on the Thrive-Thrive Matrix on the next page. But before you plot your own organization, it might be helpful to plot some other organizations to calibrate your scale. So, for example, based on what you know, where would you put Amazon, Ford, GM, HP, Penney, PepsiCo, Exxon-Mobil, Caterpillar, Goldman-Sachs, Alphabet, Chipotle, and your most significant competitor? Just plot a few to get a feel for how you're using the graph.

Now plot your own organization. You can add a directionality arrow if you think your organization may experience significant improvement or decline on either or both dimensions.

THRIVE-THRIVE MATRIX

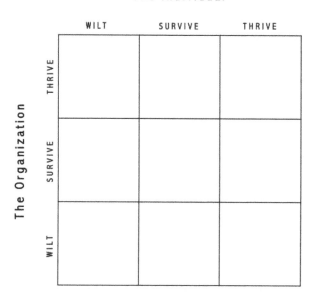

Again, it can be very useful to do this exercise with others. First, choose the four or five organizations you will use for calibrating your scales. Then, individually plot those organizations and compare and discuss. Then do the same for your organization.

REFLECTIONS FOR A CULTURE CHANGE JOURNEY

The open-ended questions below can help guide your thinking as you embark on a journey of culture change. I encourage you to date your entries, so you can track what you've learned and how it's influenced how you think about change in your organization. You may want to copy these pages, so you can always have a blank sheet to work from.

1a. What is your organization's mission or purpose?

1b. What is your personal mission or purpose? (Be honest.)

1c. What are the implications if your personal mission is or is not aligned with the company mission?

2a. Who do you directly and positively influence in the organization?

2b. Who do you directly and negatively influence in the organization?

2c. What are the implications of your particular circle of influence for a change journey?

3a. How culture savvy are you? If someone were to ask you the following questions, could you answer them?

- What is culture?

- Is culture about values or behavior?

- How does culture affect organizational outcomes?

- Can it be changed? If so, how?

- What's a good culture? What's a bad culture?

- If our numbers are good, why should we worry about culture?

3b. Given the ease and sophistication in answering the above questions, what, if anything, do you need to do to increase your culture savvy?

4a. Where are you (we) now? (Use the earlier assessment tools alone, or even better, with others.)

4b. What are the implications of your current status for a culture change effort? Favorable, unfavorable? Use a burning platform approach? Use a pursue the dream approach? Any other thoughts?

5. How can you document in a way that will be convincing to others the current status of your culture? What data can you collect? What data would be persuasive?

6a. Who in your direct circle of influence can you discuss your ideas with?

6b. Who can direct you to others in your organization who might be sympathetic allies?

6c. How can you meet people outside of your organization who might have useful insights and encouragement to share?

7. Who in your organization is already doing the best job you know of (or can find) in the direction of culture change you'd be inclined to pursue? (Go talk to that person!)

8a. What skills do you need to build before promoting a change? How will you build them?

8b. What skills do other members of your network have that will help promote change?

9. List several small wins you can imagine that will move you in the direction of the change journey you are hoping to make.

10a. Who should you invite to join you in your journey? Why?

10b. How do you get them to join you? What's their purpose?

Now try something! Run the experiment!

11a. What worked? What would you do again?

11b. What didn't work? What would you do differently next time?

11c. What else did you learn?

12. Re-do your answers starting at the beginning. Then take the next step. What will you try now?

ENDNOTES

[i.] C. Worley, *The Agility Factor*, Wiley, 2014.

[ii] V. Claar, "The Urgency of Poverty and the Hope of Genuinely Fair Trade," *Journal of Markets & Morality* (Spring 2013): 274. GDP figures from J. Bradford DeLong, "Estimates of World GDP, One Million B.C.–Present."

[iii] See: The 2010 Shift Index-EdgePerspectives; available at John Hagel III, John Seely Brown, Duleesha Kulasooriya, Dan Elbert, 2010. Measuring the forces of long-term change: The 2010 shift index.

[iv] Bart van Ark (2016). US productivity slips for first time in three decades. *Financial Times*. Retrieved from www.ft.com.

[v] Sisodia, R., and Sheth, J., *Firms of Endearment: How World-Class Companies Profit from Passion and Purpose* (2nd Edition), 2014.

[vi] See: http://fortune.com/2014/05/31/mba-popular-masters-degree/.

[vii] *2017 Deloitte Global Human Capital Trends, Rewriting the rules for the digital age*: 2017 Deloitte global human capital trends. Deloitte University Press. Retrieved from www2.deloitte.com.

viii Ralph A. Clevenger (2016, July 11). Tip of the Iceberg. St. Louise de Marillac. Cited in Shein, E; *Organizational Culture and Leadership*, 5th edition, Wiley, 2017; pg.29–30.

ix See Sheridan, R., *Joy, Inc.: How We Built a Workplace People Love;* Kindle Edition; pages 20–23.

x Patrnchak, J., *The Engaged Enterprise, A Field Guide for the Serving – Leader*, 2016.

xi See: Ancona, D., *Stronger Together: Building Distributed Leadership*, video available at https://www.youtube.com/watch?v=tvh0xeodWys& feature=youtu.be.

xii Sheridan, R., *Joy, Inc.: How We Built a Workplace People Love;* Kindle Edition: p. 143.

xiii *Firms of Endearment*, page 172 in the Kindle edition.

xiv https://www.inc.com/marcel-schwantes/these-10-leadership-habits-have-been-found-in-the-worlds-best-leaders.html.

xv Marquet, L. David, *Turn the Ship Around*, Portfolio/Penguin, 2012.

xvi See: "The Conservative Case for Unions," *The Atlantic*, July/August 2017, pg. 16.

xvii *Firms of Endearment*, page 35.

xviii *Firms of Endearment*, pg. 69.

xix Schein, E., *Organizational Culture and Leadership*, page 30–31.

xx Schein, E., *Organizational Culture and Leadership*, pg 16.

xxi Cartoon by Banx. Cited in Torben Rick. (2016). *Corporate culture will need to be both resilient and agile.* Meliorate.

xxii Christensen, C.; Allworth, J.; Dillon, K.; *How Will You Measure Your Life?* 2012.

xxiii Alan G. Robinson, & Dean M. Schroeder. (2006). *Ideas are free: how the idea revolution is liberating people and transforming organizations.* Berrett-Koehler.

xxiv For a detailed discussion of CHG culture, see: *Employee Voice: Foundation to the Scaffolding of CHG Healthcare's Culture Journey;* M. Pacanowsky, S. Scheller Arsht, A. Mackey, B.K. Baxter, L. Banks, R.T. Henage, P. Ingle, J. Manship, A. Martin, J. McGovern, A. Scott; *Organizational Dynamics* (2017).

RECOMMENDED RESOURCES

Adizes, I. (1988). *Corporate lifecycles: How and why corporations grow and die and what to do about it.* Eaglewood Cliffs, NJ: Prentice Hall.

Adizes, I. (2004). *Managing corporate lifecycles: An updated and expanded look at the classic work corporate lifecycles.* Santa Barbara, CA: The Adizes Institute Publishing.

Ancona, D.G., & Bresman, H. (2007). *X-teams: How to build teams that lead, innovate, and succeed.* Boston, MA: Harvard Business School Press.

The Arbinger Institute. (2010). *Leadership and self-deception: Getting out of the box.* San Francisco, CA: Berrett-Koehler.

The Arbinger Institute. (2008). *The anatomy of peace: Resolving the heart of conflict.* San Francisco, CA: Berrett-Koehler.

The Arbinger Institute. (2016). *The outward mindset: Seeing beyond ourselves.* Oakland, CA: Berrett-Koehler.

Bock, L. (2015). *Work rules! Insights from inside Google that will transform how you live and lead.* New York, NY: Twelve.

Buckingham, M., & Coffman, C. (1999). *First, break all the rules: What the world's greatest managers do differently.* New York, NY: Simon & Schuster.

Cain, S. (2012). *Quiet: The power of introverts in a world that can't stop talking.* Danvers, MA: Crown Publishing Group.

Chapman, B., & Sisodia, R. (2015). *Everybody matters: The extraordinary power of caring for your people like family.* New York, NY: Penguin Random House, LLC.

Christensen, C.M. (1997). *The innovator's dilemma: When new technologies cause great firms to fail.* Cambridge, MA: President and Fellows of Harvard College.

Collins, J. (2001). *Good to great: Why some companies make the leap and others don't.* New York, NY: HarperCollins.

Collins, R. (2014). *Wiki management. A revolutionary new model for a rapidly changing and collaborative world.* New York, NY: AMACOM.

Conley, C. (2007). *Peak: How great companies get their mojo from Maslow.* San Francisco, CA: Jossey-Bass.

De Geus, A. (1997). *The living company: Habits for survival in a turbulent business environment.* Boston, MA: Harvard Business School Press.

Denning, S. (2010). *The leader's guide to radical management: Reinventing the workplace for the 21st century.* San Francisco, CA: Jossey-Bass.

Dutton, J.E. (2003). *Energize your workplace: How to create and sustain high-quality connections at work.* San Francisco, CA: Jossey-Bass.

Dweck, C. (2006). *Mindset: The new psychology of success.* New York, NY: Random House, Inc.

Edmonson, A.C. (2012). *Teaming: How organizations learn, innovate, and compete in the knowledge economy.* San Francisco, CA: John Wiley & Sons.

Fredrickson, B.L. (2009). *Positivity: Top-notch research reveals the upward spiral that will change your life.* New York, NY: Random House, Inc.

Grenny, J. (2013). *Influencer: The new science of leading change.* New York, NY: McGraw-Hill Company.

Havard, A. (2007). *Virtuous leadership: An agenda for personal excellence.* Strongsville, OH: Scepter Publishers.

Hoffman, B.G. (2012). *American icon: Alan Mulally and the fight to save Ford Motor Company.* New York, NY: Crown Publishing Group.

Hoffman, B.G. (2007). *Red teaming: How your business can conquer the competition by challenging everything.* New York, NY: Penguin Random House, LLC.

Jackson, M.C. (2003). *Systems thinking: Creative holism for managers.* San Francisco, CA: John Wiley & Sons.

Johnson, B. (1992). *Polarity management: Identifying and managing unsolvable problems.* Amherst, MA: HRD Press.

Kegan, R., & Lahey, L.L. (2016). *An everyone culture: Becoming a deliberately developmental organization.* Brighton, MA: Harvard Business Review Press.

Kegan, R., & Lahey, L.L. (2009). *Immunity to change: How to overcome it and unlock the potential in yourself and your organization.* Brighton, MA: Harvard Business School Publishing.

Kirkpatrick, D. (2011). *Beyond empowerment: The age of the self-managed organization.* Sacramento, CA: Morning Star Self-Management Institute.

Koch, C.G. (2007). *The science of success: How market–based management built the world's largest private company.* Hoboken, NJ: John Wiley & Sons.

Koestenbaum, P. & Block, P. (2001). *Freedom and accountability at work: Applying philosophic insight to the real world.* San Francisco, CA: Jossey-Bass/Pfeiffer.

Krogh, G.V., Ichijo, K., & Nonaka, I. (2000). *Enabling knowledge creation: How to unlock the mystery of tacit knowledge and release the power of innovation.* Oxford, United Kingdom: Oxford University Press.

Lencioni, P. (2002). *The five dysfunctions of a team: A leadership fable.* San Francisco, CA: Jossey-Bass.

Marquet, L.D. (2012). *Turn the ship around! How to create leadership at every level.* Austin, TX: Greenleaf Book Group Press.

Martyn, M., & Crowell, B. (2012). *Own the gap.* Tualatin, Oregon: SISU Press.

Morieux, Y., & Tollman, P. (2014). *Six simple rules: How to manage complexity without getting complicated.* Boston, MA: Boston Consulting Group.

Nonaka, I., & Takeuchi, H. (1995). *The knowledge-creating company: How Japanese companies create the dynamics of innovation.* Oxford, United Kingdom: Oxford University Press.

Patterson, K., Grenny, J., & McMillan, R. (2002). *Crucial conversations: Tools for talking when stakes are high.* New York, NY: McGraw-Hill Company.

Quinn, R.E. (2015). *The positive organization.* Oakland, CA: Berrett-Koehler Publishers.

Rogers, E.M. (2003). *Diffusion of innovation* (5th ed.). New York, NY: Simon & Schuster.

Sackmann, S.A., & Stiftung, B. (2006). *Success factor: corporate culture: Developing a corporate culture for high performance and long-term competitiveness.* Gütersloh: Die Deutsche Bibliothek.

Schein, E.H. (1985). *Organizational culture and leadership*. San Francisco, CA: Jossey-Bass.

Senge, P.M. (2006). *The fifth discipline: The art and practice of the learning organization*. New York, NY: Doubleday.

Sheridan, R. (2013). *Joy, inc.: How we built a workplace people love*. New York, NY: Penguin Group.

Shorris, E. (1981). *The oppressed middle politics of middle management: Scenes from corporate life*. Garden City, NY: Anchor Press Doubleday.

Sull, D., & Eisenhardt, K.M. (2015). *Simple rules: How to thrive in a complex world*. New York, NY: Houghton Mifflin Harcourt Publishing Company.

Surowieicki, J. (2004). *The wisdom of crowds*. New York, NY: First Anchor Books.

Trompenaars, F., & Hampden-Turner, C. (2012). *Riding the waves of culture: Understanding diversity in global business*. New York, NY: McGraw Hill Company.

Weinzweig, A. (2013). *A lapsed anarchist's approach to managing ourselves*. Ann Arbor, MI: Zingerman's Press.

Whiting, K., & Whiting, V. (2011). *In pain we trust: A conversation between mother and son on the journey from sickness to health*. New York, NY: Blooming Twig Books.

Worley, C., Williams, T., & Lawler III, E.E., (2014). *The agility factor*. San Francisco, CA: Jossey-Bass.

Worline, M.C., & Dutton, J.E. (2017). *Awaking compassion at work: The quiet power that elevates people and organizations*. Oakland, CA: Berrett-Koehler.

ABOUT THE CENTER FOR INNOVATIVE CULTURES

The Center for Innovative Cultures is housed in the Bill and Vieve Gore School of Business at Westminster College. Our mission—inspired by the insights and work of Bill and Vieve Gore—is to help organizations thrive by unleashing the talent, passion, and potential of people at work.

To that end, we are constantly trying to learn about what Thriving Organizations are doing and how they are doing it, so that we can share these learnings with interested and committed organizations who want to enhance their cultural excellence.

The Center offers events for executive teams and HR and OD and cultural specialists, as well as workshops for beginning to midcareer leaders who want practical tools they can use to bring about a thriving culture in their department or function. We also offer an online survey—"The Survey of Thriving Organizational Cultures"—based on the ideas in this book.

For more information, please see our website at www.innovativecultures.org.

ABOUT THIS BOOK

Our intention is to regularly update the information in this book. We welcome readers' suggestions. If you have insightful commentary that you think might productively be included, please let us know. Similarly, if you work for a Thriving Organization and could see a case study of your organization as part of this book, please let us know that as well.

You can send an e-mail with your suggestions to innovativecultures.westminstercollege.edu.

INDEX